# Lifestyles
## *of the*
# Remnant

## Keavin Hayden

REVIEW AND HERALD® PUBLISHING ASSOCIATION
HAGERSTOWN, MD 21740

The author assumes full responsibility for the accuracy of all facts and quotations as cited in this book.

This book was
Edited by Gerald Wheeler
Copyedited by Jocelyn Fay and James Cavil
Cover design by Genesis Design/Bryan Gray
Designed by Emily Harding
Electronic makeup by Shirley M. Bolivar
Typeset: Usherwood Book 11/14

PRINTED IN U.S.A.

05 04 03 02 01          5 4 3 2 1

**R & H Cataloging Service**
Hayden, Ronald Keavin, 1960-
     Lifestyles of the remnant.

     1. Lifestyle—Seventh-day Adventists.   2. Seventh-day Adventists.
3. Christian life.   I. Title.

286.732

ISBN 0-8280-1568-6

# Dedication

I dedicate this book to the four greatest gifts God has ever bestowed upon my wife and me—our four daughters.

To Sara Elizabeth, Mary Ellen, Emily Ruth, and Lydia Danielle.

May the grace of our loving Jesus lead each of you to a balanced life of committed service to Him. Thank you for the happiness each of you has brought to our lives.

"God's cause at this time is in special need of men and women who possess Christlike qualifications for service, executive ability, and a large capacity for work, who have kind, warm, sympathetic hearts, sound common sense, and unbiased judgment; who will carefully weigh matters before they approve or condemn, and who can fearlessly say No, or Yea and Amen; who, because they are sanctified by the Spirit of God, practice the words, 'All ye are brethren,' striving constantly to uplift and restore fallen humanity."

—Ellen G. White, *Manuscript Releases,* vol. 2, p. 88.

# Books by Keavin Hayden:

*Saving Blood* (Pacific Press)
*The Shaking Among God's People*
*Truth That Matters* (Pacific Press)

To order, call 1-800-765-6955.

Visit our Web site at *www.reviewandherald.com* for information on other Review and Herald products.

# Contents

# Abbreviations

| | |
|---|---|
| AA | *The Acts of the Apostles* |
| BE | *Bible Echo* |
| CC | *Conflict and Courage* |
| CD | *Counsels on Diet and Foods* |
| CG | *Child Guidance* |
| CH | *Counsels on Health* |
| COL | *Christ's Object Lessons* |
| CT | *Counsels to Parents, Teachers, and Students* |
| CW | *Counsels to Writers and Editors* |
| DA | *The Desire of Ages* |
| ED | *Education* |
| Ev | *Evangelism* |
| EW | *Early Writings* |
| GCB | *General Conference Bulletin* |
| GW | *Gospel Workers* |
| HS | *Historical Sketches* |
| MB | *Thoughts From the Mount of Blessing* |
| 1MCP | *Mind, Character, and Personality,* vol. 1 (2MCP for vol. 2) |
| MM | *The Ministry of Healing* |
| 1MR | Ellen G. White *Manuscript Releases,* vol. 1 (2MR, etc., for vols. 2-21) |
| OHC | *Our High Calling* |
| PP | *Patriarchs and Prophets* |
| PUR | *Pacific Union Recorder* |
| RH | *Review and Herald* |
| SC | *Steps to Christ* |
| SL | *The Sanctified Life* |
| 1SM | *Selected Messages,* book 1 (2SM, etc., for books 2, 3) |
| ST | *Signs of the Times* |
| 1T | *Testimonies for the Church,* vol. 1 (2T, etc., for vols. 2-9) |
| TM | *Testimonies to Ministers* |
| YI | *Youth's Instructor* |

# Introduction

This book is about church standards. Because standards have in the past been such a controversial topic, a friend told me that to admit this up front would turn off many potential readers. But this negative reaction to the subject is exactly why I have for a long time now had a burden to write such a book.

I personally like to refer to them as "Bible standards" rather than "church standards." If we are Bible Christians, then everything we incorporate into our lives should have its foundation in the Bible. A generation is now developing within the remnant church who say "Sir, we would see Jesus" (John 12:21). Orthodoxy—that is, to accept something on the basis of church tradition—will never be good enough reason for them to change their course of action. They must be intelligently shown from the Word, the ultimate revelation of Jesus Christ. Though many will condemn this generation for their unorthodoxy, we should actually commend them for their anti-hypocrisy. Thank God, they are challenging us all to "study to shew [ourselves] approved unto God," workers "that needeth not to be ashamed, rightly dividing the word of truth" (2 Tim. 2:15).

As I have conducted a revival ministry within the Seventh-day Adventist Church during the past few years I have sensed the need for a book that would give lifestyle standards a fresh impetus among our people. So often we have presented the topic in a legalistic "do it or lose your salvation" way. No wonder we tend to be gun-shy when someone brings up the topic. My own experience has taught me that this traditional approach not only stifles the joy of our salvation but also limits our creative ability to witness to those who are different than ourselves. It inhibits us in meeting and identifying with people on their level.

We need information that will revive our hearts and get us excited once again about serving Jesus Christ in the way we live. Then people will know we have been with Him. "And ye also shall bear witness, because ye have been with me from the beginning" (John 15:27).

However, my initial attempts at writing this book proved extremely challenging. I found that I too tended to make my personal opinions and convictions the standard. But that is not what I want to do. I simply desire to present the principles from inspired writings and then allow the reader to draw his or her own conclusions. Thus I present many things that I believe to be the principle of the matter, even though it may not reflect my present position—that is to say, how I carry it out in my own life. But, thank God, I am not the standard. Jesus is as He reveals Himself to us personally through the biblical images. I can honestly say I have tried my best to separate my personal convictions from the book itself. At times I may have failed to accomplish this goal, and if so, then I want to ask the readers' forgiveness beforehand.

My prayer is that each will give due consideration to what is within these pages and then, for final guidance, look to the greatest standard of holy living that ever walked this earth, the Man Jesus Christ. The closer we can come to living by the principles that actuated His life, the happier ours will be. And the more effective witnesses we will become for Him.

May His Spirit now lead you as you consider lifestyles of the remnant.

—*Keavin Hayden*

*Chapter One*
# The Greatest Standard

The last call for boarding had been made. As I made my way to the gate, I noticed a common scene in an international airport—a young woman saying goodbye to her parents. Normally such a thing would not have caught my attention, but as I witnessed the flood of emotion between them, I stopped. I wasn't too surprised when the mother emotionally bade her daughter farewell. However, the thing that gripped my heart was seeing tears well up in the eyes of the father.

As I boarded the plane I continued to think about the experience. Then I thought about what it must have been like that day when Jesus, with suitcases in hand, said farewell to His loved ones in heaven as He left for earth. No doubt it must have been quite a scene as the angels wept with sorrow while kissing their beloved Commander goodbye. But the real heartbreaker came as the Son turned to His Father and said, "Goodbye, Father; I'll miss You." Surely only the eternal Godhead will ever be able to comprehend fully the emotional trauma the eternal Father must have gone through as He watched His Son leave the heavenly courts.

But why did Jesus make the trip? And why did the Father let Him go? Because of a thing called love. Not the so-called psychedelic love exploited in the sixties, or the selfish love of humanity that attempts to get something in return. Rather, it was the infinite love of God that He displayed in His condescension to save fallen, degraded humanity.

Such infinite love can be comprehended only through the "infinite sacrifice of Christ" (see 9T 126). Only as we begin to grasp what it cost God to save us will His love then spiritually transform us. "Christ sacrificed everything for man in order to make it possible for him to gain heaven" (3T 481). "Remember that Christ risked all. For our redemption, heaven itself was imperiled" (COL 196). And He made His great sacrifice for us while we were yet hostile to Him (Rom. 5:8). The Bible teaches that those who truly understand this will love God because He first loved them. The goodness of God will lead them to repentance. They will grow to love and honor God so much that they will sacrifice anything He asks of them, even life itself, because "they loved not their lives unto the death" (Rev. 12:11).

Such God-inspired love knows no fear or favor. It doesn't choose to sacrifice only when it is convenient or popular to do so. On the contrary, it is fearless in breaking customs and traditions if that is what is necessary to bring the life into conformity to God's will. It constantly seeks to do those things "pleasing in his sight" (1 John 3:22).

## Loving the Saints

But it is not only love for God that His remnant people will possess; it is love for one another as well. "Hereby perceive we the love of God, because he laid down his life for us: and we ought to lay down our lives for the brethren" (1 John 3:16). "We know that we have passed from death unto life, because we love the brethren" (verse 14). Many live as though they interpret this to mean that we should lay down our lives for those who agree with us. But once again, such behavior is not godly love, but human selfishness. Godlike love is not partial. It seeks to benefit all according to the eternal value that God has placed upon them. The golden rule knows no barriers of race, religion, or gender.

True love will also lead its possessor to have a noncritical, merciful attitude toward those who do not follow the right. Micah 6:8 says: "He hath shewed thee, O man, what is good; and what doth the Lord require of thee, but to do justly, and to love mercy, and to walk humbly with thy God?" Notice that it instructs us (1) to "Do justly"—that is, to do right because it is right. This will always lead us to listen conscientiously to that still small voice of conviction as it impresses us to implement needed changes in our lives. It tells us (2) to "love mercy." This means that we should not judge others. "That is, do not set yourself up as a standard. Do not make your opinions, your views of duty, your interpretations of scripture, a criterion for others, and . . . [then] condemn them if they do not [match] your ideal. Do not criticize others" (MB 124).

So while the followers of Christ will be "true to duty as the needle to the pole" (Ed 57), they will not look down their noses at others who do not share their convictions. And finally, it says (3) to "walk humbly with thy God." True Christians will never consider themselves better than anyone else. That is because they do not measure themselves by others, but rather by that greatest standard, the love of Jesus Christ. A man or woman who truly walks with God cannot help being humble. They will love others as Christ has loved them.

Perhaps this was the thought that the apostle was trying to express when he penned those immortal words: "Though I speak with the tongues of men and of angels, and have not [love], I am become as sounding brass, or a tinkling cymbal" (1 Cor. 13:1). "If I had the gift of predicting the future and could understand all science and fathom all knowledge, or if I had so much faith that I could move mountains, but didn't have love, I would be worthless. If I gave everything I had to the church and had enough money to feed the world, or if I became a martyr by being burned to death for Christ, but didn't have love, all such acts would count for nothing. Love is patient and kind. It doesn't envy, and it doesn't focus on itself or puff up with its own importance. Love is never rude nor does it behave unbecomingly. It's not interested in its own advantages. It doesn't keep a record of wrongs. Love thinks the best. Love doesn't enjoy evil, but finds joy in truth. Love bears all things, believes all things, hopes for all things, and endures all things. Love will not fail. There are three important things in life: Faith in God, hope for the future and Christ-like love, but the greatest of these is love" (verses 2-13, Clear Word).

So we see that love is the prerequisite for anything in this life that is of any value with God. If such characteristics of love do not intermingle with all that we say and do, our life will be worthless. One could even add, "And if I kept all the other standards that the Word of God commanded me, but didn't have the biblical principle of love abiding in my heart, then I have yet to truly grasp the concept of what it means to be a Christian." For to be Christlike is to be saturated in heart and mind with His love, a love for conforming to His commandments as well as a love for reaching out to those who despise them.

## "If You Love Me"

L ove is a word that we often use like a lump of Play-Doh, shaping it into anything we want and still calling it love. Because we cannot read the motives of even our own hearts, selfishness often disguises itself as love. We may even excuse blatant disobedience to God's directions as to how one should live under the pretense of love.

But Joshua of old made it very clear that to love God is to obey Him: "But take diligent heed to do the commandment and the law, which Moses the servant of the Lord charged you, to love the Lord your God, and to walk in all his ways, and to keep his commandments, and to cleave unto him, and to serve him with all your heart and with all your soul" (Joshua 22:5). Wasn't this what Jesus Himself was really trying to get across when He said: "If ye love me, keep my commandments" (John 14:15)? Though obedience will not always produce a love for Christ, a love for Christ will always result in the keeping of the commandments.

It is this love-response relationship with Christ that causes us to seek to conform our lives to His will. "When Christ dwells in the heart, the soul will be so filled with His love, with the joy of communion with Him, that it will cleave to Him; and in the contemplation of Him, self will be forgotten. Love to Christ will be the spring of action. Those who feel the restraining love of God, do not ask how little may be given to meet the requirements of God; they do not ask for the lowest standard, but aim at perfect conformity to the will of their Redeemer. With earnest desire they yield all and manifest an interest proportionate to the value of the object which they seek. A profession of Christ without this deep love is mere talk, dry formality, and heavy drudgery" (SC 44, 45).

Yet God is reasonable in what He requires of His creatures. Consider the apostle Paul. He never lowered the standard in order to accommodate his fallen nature or became discouraged because he often fell short of it. He said: "Ever since I met Jesus Christ I have wanted to know Him better and to experience the renewing power of His resurrection. . . . I've not achieved a state of flawless perfection, but as I strive to copy Him, my fellowship with Him continues to deepen. So I keep pushing ahead, going after what Christ had in mind for me when He first got hold of me. I certainly don't consider myself as having reached the divine standard of complete Christ-likeness. However, there is one thing I have done and will continue to do, and that is to forget things that are in the past and to look ahead toward the spiritual goal held out to us by God who is calling us heavenward through Jesus Christ His Son. . . . In the meantime, at whatever growth stage we find ourselves, let's keep the same objective in view that we had when we first found Christ" (Phil. 3:10-16, Clear Word).

The devil is forever trying to make God look unreasonable in His requirements of us. He subtly suggests that God sets impossibly high Christian standards through His law, and then commands that we must somehow pole vault to it or be lost. While without doubt the only acceptable standard to God appears in His holy law, He has also devised a fair way to help us attain to it. God sets no arbitrary standards. He expects from us only what we have. "For if there be first a willing mind, it is accepted according to that a man hath, and not according to that he hath not" (2 Cor. 8:12). Though in context the passage involves stewardship, the same principle applies to all God's dealings with us. He is well aware of our various backgrounds, circumstances, and disabilities. The actual level of performance that you achieve, I might not be able to. But if we are both giving all that we have, we each will be found perfect in Christ.

The main point we must grasp here is that we need not become discouraged when we fall short in trying to be like Jesus. "Jesus loves His children, even if they err. . . . He keeps His eye upon them, and when they do their best, calling upon God for His help, be assured the service will be accepted, although imperfect. . . . Jesus makes up for our unavoidable deficiencies" (3SM 195, 196). But note that this fact will not excuse our deliberate imperfections. "God will not accept a willfully imperfect service" (RH, Sept. 3, 1901). It is one thing to fail to measure up to the standard because we have, with good intentions, tried our best and fallen short. But it is quite another thing when a person has determined in his or her mind that the standard laid out before them is unreasonable and unattainable and therefore does not even try to live up to it. Without question those who follow such reasoning will surely fail to become like Christ in character.

Of course, nothing we do can ever earn us mileage points toward a flight to heaven. Christ paid the ticket in full at Calvary and now offers it to us as a free gift, a token of His love for us. But the person who really understands this gospel reality will, out of love and gratitude, go to the greatest lengths to serve their Redeemer obediently. Such individuals do not want God's grace merely for the pardon of their sins. They also seek that grace "for obedience to the faith among all nations, for his name" (Rom. 1:5). "Ye are my witnesses, saith the Lord, and my servant whom I have chosen" (Isa. 43:10).

## Safety Standards

It is imperative that we remember that God has not arbitrarily placed upon us standards to restrict our joy or freedom. He sets standards for His children with good reason. God loves us and doesn't want us destroyed by Satan.

Have you ever gone to a zoo and watched the lions around feeding time? The better part of the day they lazily lounge around, but at feeding time they arouse for the hunt. There you stand in front of them as they pace back and forth, staring at you through the bars. Are they simply intrigued that you've paid good money to come and watch them and so they want to put on a good show for you? No, they are looking for two things: food, and a little bend in the bars or a crack in the door of the cage so they can get through to eat you alive.

So it is with our spiritual adversary, the devil. He "as a roaring lion, walketh about, seeking whom he may devour" (1 Peter 5:8). And it is the biblical standards of our faith that keep this deadly spiritual beast from devouring us. God, in His infinite wisdom, sees the weak spots of our fallen natures that the devil can easily use for our destruction. So, because He loves us and cares for both our present and eternal welfare, He has delivered to us, through His prophets, vital counsels that will protect us.

The bottom line is that God honors our will concerning the things in which He has instructed us. It is up to us whether or not we choose to heed His counsel. Just as was the case with Adam and Eve in Eden, whether or not we accept the Lord's counsel will clearly reveal if we really place our trust in Him. Ultimately it is always an outward manifestation of a trustful, obedient attitude toward God that distinguishes between the faith of the righteous and the unrighteous.

"By faith Abraham . . . obeyed" (Heb. 11:8). The truly righteous will recognize that all standards stemming from God's law, whether they pertain to things large or small, are "holy, and just, and good" (Rom. 7:12). They will obey from the heart (Rom. 6:17).

It is out of infinite love that God delivered His counsel to us. And it is the love of God in sending us His Son that is the greatest of all standards. This alone has the power to transform and unify God's remnant. Only then can they appear "fair as the moon, clear as the sun, and terrible as an army with banners" (S. of Sol. 6:10). And "his banner over me was love" (S. of Sol. 2:4).

*Chapter Two*
# I Would Be Like Jesus

I t was one of those difficult, embarrassing moments when you just wish you could crawl under a chair or otherwise fade out of sight. At a camp meeting the ABC manager had set up a book signing for me. Such events allow me an opportunity to respond to people on a personal level. But the blessing soon turned into an author's nightmare. With about 10 people present in the store a young man came out from behind a bookshelf and publicly began denouncing me as antichrist. He intensely warned a woman I had been talking with not to listen to me. As I tried to reason with him he became more belligerent with his denunciations. It soon became apparent that the best thing for me to do was just to ignore him. The woman, however, came to my defense as she calmly talked to him and led him out of the store.

The struggles that man had with what I was teaching are not uncommon in our churches. They involve what inspired counsel means when it instructs us to develop a Christlike character. As I have investigated the matter, I have concluded that a misinterpretation of what Ellen White meant when she says we are to perfect a Christian character propels some people to take extreme positions regarding the lifestyle counsels she gave to the remnant.

In this book I want to be careful not to get so intertwined with theology that it distracts us from our focus—the principles of holy living. However, the unavoidable fact is that we can never get away from our theology. What we perceive God to be like, as well as what we think He expects of us, will always appear in our lives through what we say, what we do, and how we relate to others.

My goal here is that we "be guided by true theology and common sense" (CT 257). "Close reasoners and logical thinkers are few for the reason that false influences have checked the development of the intellect" (3T 142, 143). This is particularly true in the way many translate their theology into lifestyle. One thing is certain—extreme theology lends itself to extreme teachings and behavior concerning lifestyle issues. On the other hand, a balanced theology will most likely produce a more balanced approach to incorporating lifestyle principles into the Christian experience.

One "false influence" that puts a check on the development of the Christian's intellect is the inability to distinguish between idealism and realism. The Bible and the writings of Ellen White speak in both realms. God commissioned prophets to present absolute standards. This is idealism. Such statements act as a "schoolmaster" by showing us how far short we fall of the perfect standard (see Gal. 3:24). Through idealistic standards the Lord convinces us of our inability to meet perfectly the high claims of the law of God in our fallen, carnal state. Only as we realize this will we begin to look outside ourselves to Christ, whose substitutionary merits offer our only hope of fully satisfying what the law requires of us.

While some recognize this, others lose touch with reality and convince themselves that they can actually live the law as perfectly as Christ did. They thus create and attempt to live in an unreal world, because they fail to realize that such perfection exists only in their imagination (see 2 MCP 636). The inevitable tragedy is that such perfectionist personalities often expect everyone else, both in their family and in their church, to follow their example. When that doesn't happen they often turn critical, which results in broken homes and churches.

## "Be Ye Therefore Perfect"

So what did Jesus mean when He instructed us to "be ye therefore perfect, even as your Father which is in heaven is perfect" (Matt. 5:48)? Was He speaking idealism or realism? Ellen White enlightens us that it means that "we may be perfect in our sphere, even as God is perfect in His" (MB 77). But our sphere is still carnal, even after our conversion to Christ. As the apostle lamented: "For I know that in me (that is, in my flesh, [or carnal nature]) dwelleth no good thing" (Rom. 7:18). Ellen White declared that the carnal state of Romans 7:18 will be with us all the way to the Second

Coming (2SM 32, 33).

But God in His sphere has no such carnal condition. And neither did Jesus when He became incarnate. Even though a man, He was still God. The essence of our carnal natures is that they are not in harmony, but at enmity, with God's law (Rom. 8:7). But His nature was in total harmony with the precepts of Jehovah. Speaking of His incarnated coming, the Bible says, "Then said I, Lo, I come. . . . I delight to do thy will, O my God: yea, thy law is within my heart" (Ps. 40:7, 8).

Here is the eternal difference between God and us, as contrasted between the earthly life of Jesus and ours. We need a righteous character that meets the infinite perfection of God's character in order to gain entrance into heaven. But because of the carnal nature we received from Adam, "we cannot perfectly obey the holy law." Thus we cannot "form a righteous character [that is, a character that meets the divine standard] by obedience to God's law," the thing that we need to gain eternal life (SC 62).

We must acknowledge this fact before we will ever begin looking outside our own performance. Only then will we be prepared to accept Christ's record of meeting the perfect standard of the law as a complete substitute for our sinful life, and His atoning death on Calvary's cross as a total payment for the debt our sins incurred. The moment we do this, *Christ's character stands in place of your character, and you are accepted before God just as if you had not sinned"* (*ibid.;* italics supplied). At that moment, we by faith become recipients of eternal life.

I later found out, from the woman who helped calm the young man at my book signing, that it had been my preaching of these thoughts that had caused him to denounce me as antcihrist. He was the victim of a traditional teaching that has plagued Adventism for years—that God expects us to unite with the power of the Holy Spirit and develop in this life a character that is as absolutely perfect as Christ's. This concept also claims that we must attain such perfect sinlessness before the close of probation, or else we will be lost when Jesus comes to gather His children home.

But the truth is that this traditional view is itself the teaching of antichrist. The word *antichrist* literally means "another Christ." If fully developed, the concept will lead us to conclude that someday we won't need the intercession of Christ's substitutionary merits to stand in God's presence, because we will have become sinless enough ourselves through holy living. Many Adventists still believe that we can—and must—develop within ourselves a character good enough to gain entrance into the kingdom. But if that is possible, then all we need is the Holy Spirit to make us good enough. We really don't need Christ's substitutionary character, do we?

Jesus struck at the root of this deception in His parable of the wedding garment (see Matt. 22:1-14). *"The wedding garment is the righteousness of Christ, and represents the character of those who will be accepted* as guests for the marriage supper of the Lamb" (YI, Oct. 21, 1897). In a practical sense, what is this righteousness that He offers us? It is the perfect character He wrought out in His earthly life. When we by faith accept Him as our substitute, heaven considers His perfect, infinite character as though it were ours. Heaven accounts us as meeting the perfect, infinite standard of the divine law, even though in our lives we really don't.

Sure, our lives change and resemble more and more the righteous life that Jesus possessed. A solid definition of righteousness is "right doing" (COL 312). The gospel guides us to do right things. But because of our carnal state (even after conversion) "all our righteousnesses [right doings] are as filthy rags" (Isa. 64:6; see also 1SM 343, 344). We can meet the absolute standard of righteousness that the law demands only by faith by accepting Christ as our substitute righteousness. It will never be seen as a tangible reality in our experience. *"Christ's righteousness alone* can avail for his salvation and this is the gift of God. *This is the wedding garment* in which you may appear as a welcome guest at the marriage supper of the Lamb" (*ibid.* 331; italics supplied). Those who by faith understand this gospel truth "receive and rejoice in the imputed righteousness of Christ. They know what it means to have a change of raiment" (YI Oct. 21, 1897). The truly sanctified person does not boast of his righteousness, that is, he is never impressed with all the right things he is doing (see SL 13). And all will have their characters tested to demonstrate where their trust lies. "While those who are *self-confident, and trust in their own perfection of character,* lose their false robe of righteousness when subjected to the storms of trial, the truly righteous, who sincerely love and fear God, wear the robe of Christ's righteousness in prosperity and adversity alike" (*ibid.* 11; italics supplied).

If we deny our eternal need of Christ's substitutionary character and continue thinking that we must weave a garment of flawless character in the loom of our own carnal natures, then where are we really putting our trust? In Christ, or in what we can produce in ourselves? If we refuse the robe of righteousness that God offers us (the character Christ perfected in His humanity) and trust to our own success of self-righteous character building, then will we not inevitably attempt to gain entrance into the marriage supper of the Lamb by means of our own efforts (a human-made garment of fig leaves)? "And when the king came in to see the guests, he saw there a man which had not on a wedding garment: and he saith unto him, Friend, how camest thou in hither not having a wedding garment? And he was speechless. Then said the king to the servants, Bind him hand and foot, and take him away, and cast him into outer darkness; there shall be weeping and gnashing of teeth" (Matt. 22:11-13).

We always face the danger of becoming too focused on the exterior when trying to discern the development of true Christian character, whether it be in ourselves or others. If we do this, no doubt we run the risk Samuel did when he tried to find kingly material among Jesse's sons. We can't accurately read the motives of others, even though we often think we can. A wise person will not even try to figure out who is going to prove to be wheat and who a tare. "It may be under a rough and uninviting exterior that the pure brightness of a genuine Christian character will be revealed" (5T 81).

## Perfection of Character

Now, I don't want to be misunderstood. I'm not saying that Christians do not experience a transformation in their characters. As we become completely dependent upon Christ through justification we establish a spiritual connection that enables Him to change our hearts. He leads us to "works of righteousness, obedience" (SC 63). The more we come to love Christ, the more we will desire to be like Him in character. What I'm trying to point out, however, is that we should never expect to reach the place at which we will match His level of character perfection. Isaiah 40:25 says: "To whom then will ye liken me, *or shall I be equal?* saith the Holy One." We must always remember that even those good works that Christ creates in us still fail to meet the infinite standard of the law. There never comes a time when we stop needing Christ's character standing in place of ours. Revelation 14:6 declares that the gospel of Christ's substitutionary merits is an eternal truth, not a temporary one.

Ellen White recognized that our sanctification will never lead us to equal Christ in character. She taught that we can only echo it. "He is a perfect and holy example, given for us to imitate. *We cannot equal the pattern;* but we shall not be approved of God if we do not copy it and, according to the ability which God has given, *resemble it*" (2T 549; italics supplied). "He had a mighty influence, for He was the Son of God. We are so far beneath Him and so far deficient, that, *do the very best we can, our efforts will be poor.* . . . But why should we not educate ourselves to *come just as near to the Pattern as it is possible for us to do,* that we may have the greatest possible influence upon the people?" (*ibid.* 617, 618). Please notice that we shall not be "approved" of God if we do not have a desire to "resemble" the life of Christ.

To think we can ever match Christ's character is a blasphemous thought. "There are many, especially among those who profess holiness, who compare themselves to Christ, *as though they were equal with Him in perfection of character. This is blasphemy.* Could they obtain a view of Christ's righteousness, they would have a sense of their own sinfulness and imperfection" (RH, Mar. 15, 1887; italics supplied). When we entertain such thoughts we are no different than the little horn power of Daniel's vision who "magnified himself even to the prince of the host" (Dan. 8:11). Carry this thought a little further and we will think that at the end of time we will become holy enough to live without the mediatorial benefits of Christ's substitutionary merits. By this means we theologically usurp Christ's authority and take upon ourselves His prerogative as the divine Mediator. Think about it. Not to require Christ's substitutionary merits means that we ourselves must possess the qualifications of the Mediator. Instead of becoming like Christ, through such thoughts we become antichrist. It usually shows as we begin forcing what we believe are right standards upon others in the home and in the church.

Concerning our blasphemous thoughts of ever equaling Christ's character, the Lord says: "Humble yourselves in the sight of the Lord" (James 4:10). The Bible declares that "there is one God, and one mediator between God and men, the man Jesus Christ" (1 Tim. 2:5). It is actually on the basis of His perfect character that Christ is qualified to be our Mediator. "Christ came as the sinner's substitute to bear the guilt Himself, which justly belonged to man. *Through the perfection of His character He was accepted of the Father as a mediator for sinful man.* He only could save man by imputing to him His righteousness" (YI, Jan., 1874; italics supplied). "Upon His meditorial work [through the ministering of His righteous merits] hangs the hope of the perishing world. *No one but Christ has ever succeeded in living a perfect life, in living a pure, spotless character"* (GCB, Oct. 1, 1899; italics supplied).

The truth is that "no man can look within himself and find anything in his character that will recommend him to God, or make his acceptance sure" (ST, Aug. 22, 1892). That is why we need the robe of Christ's character to cover us. To those who trust completely in His substitutionary character of righteousness, He says: "The Father beholds not your faulty character, but He sees you as clothed in My perfection" (DA 357). It is the way things will continue all the way down to the Second Coming. We will forever be developing our characters while on earth. Speaking of the one who follows after and trusts in Christ, Ellen White stated: "He is perfecting Christian character after the divine model, . . . and this work [of becoming more like Christ] *will progress in his character until faith is lost in sight, and grace in glory* [at the Second Coming]" (ST, May 16, 1895; italics supplied). We never arrive at total, inherent character perfection. As we learned from Luther, and Luther from Paul, and Paul from Habakkuk, and Habakkuk from God, "the just shall live by faith" (see Hab. 2:4; Eph. 2:8).

In fact, Inspiration tells us that we will forever strive to be like Jesus. *"The efforts begun on earth [for perfection of Christian character] will continue through eternity"* (4T 520). Ellen White is, of course, contrasting the character we develop with the "infinitely perfect character" that was developed in the person of Jesus Christ (6T 60). It's this absolute character perfection that we will never attain to. How can finite creatures ever think they can reach the spiritual state of an infinite God? Such thoughts transformed the angel Lucifer into the demon called Satan (see Isaiah 14).

But we can be relatively perfect in our sphere by exercising the abilities God has given us to be as much like Jesus as we can. Oftentimes, though, we even get discouraged in this because we fail in our Christian standardkeeping. But we need not despair. "Do not be discouraged because you see that your character is defective. The closer you come to Jesus, the more faulty you will appear in your own eyes; for your vision will be clearer, and *your imperfections will be seen in distinct contrast with His perfect character*" (BE, Dec. 1, 1892; italics supplied).

Some may use this chapter to continue their un-Christlike behavior. But if we really sense our unworthiness and truly lament our sinful condition, we will not try to excuse our sins. Instead we will face them realistically. Our sincere attempts to live above sin indicate our repentance. Once we come to acknowledge our unavoidable deplorable condition, we shall begin to look forward to the day of glorification. It is at the great Second Advent that we shall finally realize our hope of a perfect sinless state, when our "faith is lost in sight" (ST, May 16, 1895). "Beloved, . . . it doth not yet appear what we shall be: but we know that, when he shall appear, we shall be like him; for we shall see him [by beholding we become changed] as he is" (1 John 3:2).

## Character Defined

Ellen White, though she always tried to encourage people in their character growth, was also sensible and reasonable concerning life's realities. In the last year of her life she wrote, "I do not say that I am perfect, but I am trying to be perfect. I do not expect others to be perfect; and if I could not associate with my brothers and sisters who are not perfect, I do not know what I should do" (PUR, Apr. 29, 1915).

We need to accept faulty people around us just as God does, perfect through Jesus while yet imperfect in themselves. If we do this, we shall see less to criticize. It will transform us into encouragers of the saints. Then, if we ever do have to consider their faults, it will only be in an attempt to help. Like surgeons who prior to surgery discuss a patient's problems for the sole purpose of trying to save them, we will discuss the faults of others only for the goal of ascertaining how we can help them out of their problems.

Ellen White defined character as the direction of the life, not the incidental word or action. Notice her description of the realistic process of character development that will take place in those who give their lives to God: "A change will be seen in the character, the habits, the pursuits. The contrast will be clear and decided between what they have been and what they are. *The character is revealed [defined], not by occasional good deeds and occasional misdeeds, but by the tendency [bent, direction] of the habitual words and acts*" (SC 57; italics supplied).

It is the tenor of our characters that will be changed (see TM 442). The victory we must gain is to practice these things habitually. Our only trust should be in the absolute victory of Christ's perfect life record. He never once fell to any of the things that continue to trip us up.

I bring this up because before we contemplate the standards of holy living, we first need to recognize our total dependence upon Jesus. Otherwise we might fall into the trap of thinking that our salvation ultimately depends upon our performance as we live out the divinely inspired standards. It produces a works approach toward salvation that always leads to extremes. Such religion provides us with no security, because we never feel we are doing good enough. Or it creates the most fatal deception of all—that we can become perfect within ourselves and live without fault, which in turn makes us overbearing with others who don't (see 1 John 1:8).

"By one offering He has perfected forever those who are being sanctified" (Heb. 10:14, NKJV). We avoid such extremes by realizing that because of our faith in Jesus we are already accounted as though we were perfect at every step of our sanctification process (which lasts a lifetime—see AA 560). Such an approach allows us to begin needed lifestyle changes with a sense of confidence, security, and optimism. Christ's substitution of His righteous character provides us an incubator, filled with divine grace, wherein we can grow up into Christ. It affords us room to fail and still not get discouraged. This umbrella of eternal grace sweetens our dispositions as we seek to straighten out our defective characters. And it makes us more tolerant with others over lifestyle issues, because we realize how patient God is being with us.

*Chapter Three*
# The Struggle Over Standards

Outside of theological differences, probably no other single issue has caused more disunity, or revealed just how destitute we have been of a golden rule spirit, than that of lifestyle standards. Disagreement over what kind of music is acceptable, the wearing of jewelry, styles of dress, what one should eat (or not eat), the appropriateness of drama and/or other theatrical performances, or what activities are acceptable recreation have alienated not only church members but blood relatives as well. Too often such issues have divided us into separate camps.

A pastor with more liberal views comes to a church that has traditionally had a more conservative nature. Feeling that the members need to become more open to change, he takes it upon himself to introduce a more nontraditional style of worship. As a result, the church's membership gradually dwindles because members seek another environment to worship in.

A conservative member withdraws his financial support from his local church's plans to conduct an evangelistic series because he discovered that it will use a more contemporary style of music in an attempt to reach the younger generations. Or what is even worse, a young woman stops coming to church because she found out that some of the other members have been condemning her more liberal mode of dress behind her back.

Regardless of who is right and who is wrong in such scenarios, it is the church of Jesus Christ that reaps the bitter harvest of seeds sown in discord and strife.

What is the answer to it all? Where are we to draw the line of balance? How do we achieve unity in a climate of such diversity? Well, it all comes back around to practicing the golden rule. If we are ever to have unity within our ranks, the members of the church must learn to do what Christ did. "The Lord wants His people to follow other methods than that of condemning wrong, *even though the condemnation is just.* He wants us to do something more than to hurl at our adversaries charges that only drive them farther from the truth. The work which Christ came to do in our world was *not to erect barriers,* and constantly thrust upon the people the fact that they were wrong. He who expects to enlighten a deceived people *must come near to them and labor for them in love.* He must become a center of holy influence" (GW 373; italics supplied).

Though Ellen White here primarily has in mind how we should treat those outside our ranks, it is also a great prescription for dealing with those inside the church. Without doubt, most of us always assume that our position is the right one. Oftentimes we find ourselves filled with holy zeal in thinking others need to be won to our side of the issues. But whatever our position may be, hurling condemnations and erecting barriers is not the answer. If we can simply stop doing this, it will close the door against Satan's divisive campaign in the church. And it will create a climate in which the Lord can work out the difficulties in His own time and in His own way.

## Silly Contentions

Sometimes the things over which we divide ourselves are really silly. A story tells of a young preacher who moved to a new church in the southern part of the United States. Soon after his arrival he decided to visit some of the nonattending members.

A few years earlier a project to renovate the sanctuary had divided the congregation. The major point of disagreement had involved which side of the church the piano should go on. The factions drew lines and began to argue. As a result, several of the members stopped coming to church because they were outvoted.

The young pastor made his first visit to the home of one of the disgruntled former members. As he began talking with the old man, the subject of the piano debate came up. Trying to recall the exact events, the old man called out to his wife, who was working in the kitchen, "Hey, honey! Which side of dat church wuz it dat I wonted dat dar pianer on?"

Sounds ridiculous, doesn't it? Yet if we would only stop to consider some of the issues that have splintered some of our congregations we would find that we have been involved in equally ridiculous contentions ourselves. It's amazing how quickly we overlook all the things we do have in common as a people, such as the 27 fundamental doctrines, and will focus on disagreements about lifestyle issues to the point of creating division in the church.

Often it's not so much the specific topic that is really the issue. The real problem is our stubborn, un-Christlike hearts. Oftentimes the controversies are smoke screens behind which we hide our unconverted souls. And in most cases, when we win the arguments we lose the relationship. The truth is that "if pride and selfishness were laid aside, five minutes would remove most difficulties" between us (EW 119). Selfishness flourishes when people are "wedded to [their] own opinion and extol [their] own judgment above that of others" (4T 126).

If we are not careful we can become so religious that we become insensitive to the God-given rights others have concerning their convictions of conscience. Paul protested this violation of liberty when he said, "For why should my freedom be judged by another's conscience?" (1 Cor. 10:29, NIV). Narrow, judgmental attitudes may blunt our holier emotions, such as compassion and mercy. Having become so dogmatic and adamant that our chosen standards of living are correct, we begin a kind of inquisition that writes off all who do not view things the way we do. But while in the days of Christ the Lord accepted many who lived outside Israel's established standards, He removed Himself from the self-righteous and left them with their own standards. Now having only a "form of godliness," they lost the power of true godliness to be found in mercy and compassion. They even began to consider such attributes as unnecessary.

Now, I'm not trying to do away with standards. All I'm attempting to point out is that if we are not careful, we can, while thinking we are God's Elijah for a particular cause, easily violate the greatest standard of all—love. How can we come close to others if we are constantly trying to push our agendas onto them? The truth is, when the Holy Spirit really gets hold of us we would rather yield our opinion than cause anyone to stumble unnecessarily over our course, even if we think we are in the right.

Once at a meeting an individual approached Ellen White, informing her that "some were in trial because Sister White wore gold." She explained the details of the incident and how she practiced the golden rule in dealing with it. "Some time before, I had received a present of a little open-faced, gold watch. It was very ancient in appearance, and certainly never would have been worn for its beauty. I carried it because it was a good timekeeper. But in order to avoid all occasion for any to stumble, I sold the watch, and I would recommend that others follow a similar course. This is in harmony with the teaching of the apostle Paul, who says: 'Wherefore, if meat make my brother to offend, I will eat no flesh while the world standeth, lest I make my brother to offend'" (HS 123).

Is this not appropriate counsel for our more liberal elements within Adventism who are seeking to change the traditional ways of doing things? The principle demands our careful consideration, because if, by our headstrong course, we cause any to stumble when we could have pursued a different course toward them, we sin against Jesus Christ in the person of that member (see 1 Cor. 8:12). "Woe unto the world because of offences! for it must needs be that offences come; but woe to that man by whom the offence cometh!" (Matt. 18:7). In other words, if change is necessary, God will bring it around by other means than appointing us to go around trying to cram it down people's throats! And God forbid that we be found doing it. (This of course does not mean that we cannot share our convictions in an appropriate, unforceful, Christlike way.)

On the other hand, we would do well as a people not to condemn so quickly and to reject some new idea or practice just because it conflicts with the church's tradition. Such a spirit will inevitably lead us to the same place it did the Jews in Christ's day, and our own Adventist forebears in 1888. "There are those who oppose everything that is not in accordance with their own ideas, and by so doing they endanger their eternal interest as verily as did the Jewish nation in their rejection of Christ" (CW 35, 36). "Those who think that they will never have to give up a cherished view, never have occasion to change an opinion, will be disappointed. As long as we hold to our own ideas and opinions with determined persistency, we cannot have the unity for which Christ prayed" (*ibid.* 37). Just as has happened in the past, those who hold to traditional, conservative views face the danger of finding undue fault with those who might seek to do things differently than they would.

## The Solution Is Christ

Ellen White warns us that we should be weeding out of our characters the natural tendency to focus on the wrong everyone is doing. She said that "all the religion many have is to pick flaws. I once knew a lady whose religion was of just this character, and in her family she was so overbearing that they could hardly live with her. A tent-meeting was held near the place where she lived, but instead of taking hold to help those who were laboring very hard in the meetings, or to receive help herself, this woman stood back to criticise. On returning to the house one day, I found her searching my trunk to see if there was not some article of clothing in it that she could condemn. We shall ever have just such people to deal with in this world. *But if we do not enter too much into particulars,* they will have no excuse for indulging their natural disposition [to criticize]. It is a marvel to me what patience the Lord has with such crooked material. But He has ordained *that by the clear presentation of truth all can be brought into love and harmony"* (HS 123; italics supplied).

Did you catch that last sentence? "By the clear presentation of truth all can be brought into love and harmony." It will take more than just argument to effect true and lasting change in someone's life. They must see Jesus and fall in love with Him. *"We must present the principles of truth,* and let them work upon the hearts of the people. We may pick the leaves from a tree as often as we please, but this will not cause the tree to die; the next season the leaves will come out again as thick as before. But strike the ax at the root of the tree, and not only will the leaves fall off themselves, but the tree will die. Those who accept the truth, in the love of it, will die to the world, and will become meek and lowly in heart like their divine Lord. *Just as soon as the heart is right, the dress, the conversation, the life will be in harmony with the Word of God"* (*ibid.* 123, 124; italics supplied).

If we really have a burden to make genuine, effective changes in others, we must present to them "Jesus Christ, and him crucified" (1 Cor. 2:2). Here is the real key to leading others to lasting change.

Notice that "if we can awaken an interest in men's minds that will cause them to fix their eyes on Christ, *we may step aside,* and ask them only to continue to fix their eyes upon the Lamb of God. They thus receive their lesson. Whosoever will come after Me, let him deny himself, and take up his cross, and follow me. *He whose eyes are fixed on Jesus will leave all.* He will die to selfishness" (21 MR 37).

To promote lifestyle standards without presenting Christ will accomplish nothing more than to increase the population of Pharisees within the church. In doing so, under the guise of holiness, we "compass sea and land to make one proselyte, and when he is made, [we] make him twofold more the child of hell than [ourselves]" (Matt. 23:15).

Without doubt we will continue to struggle in the church over standards. As a sad matter of fact, the struggle is probably going to increase as we draw closer to the end of time. But let us seek not to displease God as we find ourselves forced to deal with such issues. Instead, let us with compassionate hearts draw close to those we want to help. Let us give them room to live out their convictions, just as we desire they do for us. But most of all, let's seek to turn their eyes away from the human elements in the church to Jesus. Then we will watch the amazing transformations of lives that only the Lord can create.

## Chapter Four

# Safety Principles for God's Workers

I ncorporating biblical principles into the life, within the context of the gospel, is one of the greatest challenges that confronts Christians today. We will discover the secret to success only as we enter into the laboratory of our relationship with God. As we understand and experience more and more of the love that God has for us personally, and respond to that love by trying to make His standards our own, we mature in the gospel. A major key in helping us stay balanced while accomplishing this task is to understand the difference between principles and rules.

God communicates the standards of His law in terms of both principles and rules. A rule is an absolute guideline that is to be carried out exactly the same way, every time, regardless of circumstances. Rules are limited in their scope and application. While rules may apply to people in one culture of the world they may not apply to those in another. Also, rules may cover one group of people while another group may have special exemption from them. For example, rules in a school may be binding upon students, but not faculty.

A principle is a more general guideline that can adapt to changing circumstances. Unlike rules, principles are universal and allow for no special privileges. While rules are subject to amendment or elimination, principles can never be discarded. They only change in their application to meet varying situations.

Humanity has always preferred to follow rules because it requires little thought. To apply a principle, however, demands greater reasoning ability. Yet it is God's highest desire for us to live as Jesus did through the application of biblical principles.

In accordance with His goal, He has given us the testimonies of His Spirit through Ellen White to help teach us how to apply biblical principles. "The Word of God abounds *in general principles for the for-*

*mation of correct habits of living,* and the Testimonies, general and personal, have been calculated to call their attention more especially to these *principles"* (4T 323; italics supplied). To understand and teach obedience to the Word of God, based upon principle, is the very essence of true education. Such learning leads to the intelligent exercise of one's own free will rather than just making decisions because of force, peer pressure, or any other means of manipulation. "It is the work of true education to develop this power [the power of an individual to think and do for themselves], to train the youth to be thinkers, and not mere reflectors of other men's thought" (Ed 17).

Servitude to human law results from following rules. God's law, the Ten Commandments, consists of 10 concise principles. Yet at times He has to lay down rules for His people to follow in order to meet them in their immature spiritual state.

That's the way it was with the Israelites as they came out of Egypt during the Exodus. While slaves they had become accustomed to following the rules of their Egyptian taskmasters. But after their deliverance from bondage God gave them the 10 principles of His ten commandment law (see Ex. 20:1-17). Though they promised to obey these principles, they were still too immature in their spiritual experience to know how to apply them in life's complex situations. So in order to meet them where they were, God gave them stated rules based on those divine principles. Such rules became known as the laws of Moses. It was God's design that as His people matured in following these rules, they might become acquainted with the principles on which the rules had been based. Then they would be better able to carry out those principles as they encountered varying circumstances.

Likewise, the standards Ellen White reveals in her writings she many times presents as established rules based on biblical principles. God's purpose in giving them was that we might learn how to better incorporate biblical principles into our lives, thus making us more effective witnesses for Christ. However, the spiritually immature mind often misses the biblical principles because of its fixation and focus on the rule. Failing to realize the changing of times and /or circumstances, such individuals leap to extreme and illogical conclusions regarding lifestyle issues, all the while using a "Sister White says so" in their defense.

Failure to distinguish the important difference between principles and rules only increases the number of rules. Instead of focusing on the Ten Commandments and their logical applications, we tend to multiply and establish rules *based on our private interpretation* of those top 10 principles. The same was true in the days of Israel as they introduced rules upon rules regarding how one should keep holy the Sabbath. Such rules had become so strict during the time of Christ that even He clashed with people's personal views of what it meant to live holy lives (see Matt. 12). *So today, Adventists who fail to comply with the norm find themselves looked down upon by a rule-oriented class within the church.* My point is that we should focus on the obvious meaning of the commandments and not on people's personal interpretation of them. This would solve a lot of conflict among us regarding how Adventists should pattern their lives. In other words, *define the black and white but steer clear of legislating gray areas.*

## Commonsense Christianity

As mentioned earlier, only the spiritually mature can properly apply divine principles. Maybe we can understand better through the following example.

One can explain to small children the principle of being temperate through providing their minds and bodies with adequate amounts of sleep. Then, like the children of Israel, they may promise to obey by getting plenty of rest. But because of immaturity they have no real concept as to how much rest they need. Would you really expect them to come to you at 7:00 in the evening and tell you that, although they aren't really tired, they know they need the rest and are therefore on their way to bed? Of course not. They will play until they drop! So in order to help them follow the principle we must make a rule called "bedtime."

But I ask, Is there anything sacred about going to bed at 7:00? What if we are out with the family one night at a Bible study and don't make it home to get the children in bed until 9:00? Have we sinned because we broke the rule? No, because circumstances called for the exception. *"God wants us all to have common sense, and He wants us to reason from common sense. Circumstances alter conditions.*

*Circumstances change the relation of things"* (3SM 217; italics supplied).

Now, what about the next evening when everything is back to normal and you tell the children it's time for bed? Instead of obeying, they begin protesting on the basis that last night they stayed up until 9:00. Is their reasoning justifiable? Of course not. And why? *Because the bending of the rule when circumstances do not warrant it will inevitably lead to a compromise of the principle altogether.*

This lack of mental maturity also appeared in the early Christian church. The writer of Hebrews chastised God's people because they had been involved in a spiritual relationship with God long enough to be living by principles, yet still needed spelled-out rules to guide them. He said they should be living on the meat of the gospel experience, but instead they still required milk (see Heb. 5:12-14).

Since rules are the application of a principle according to time and circumstances, they can become outdated. Mature Christians able to apply principle are more balanced witnesses because they can properly adapt new rules to changing times and circumstances without violating principle. But persons incapable of reasoning for themselves and able to follow only a rule made by another can, with the passing of time and changing of circumstances, easily become unbalanced and make themselves ineffective witnesses for Christ. They can more easily dishonor the Lord through extreme decisions.

An example of how the application of a principle can change over time is the counsel that in educating our youth it would be useful "if girls . . . could learn to harness and drive a horse" (Ed 216, 217). It was totally appropriate and valuable counsel for the times in which Ellen White wrote it. To carry out such a rule today would, in most cases, be extreme. Yet we need not ignore such counsel, because it has an underlying and still valid principle—that it would be wise for women to be able to perform the basic duties of caring for and operating their mode of transportation.

Though obviously our salvation does not rest on our ability to maintain an automobile, such counsel shows how very interested God is in the little things of our lives. I know a young woman whose father's car overheated as she drove it one summer day. Seeking to add more water to the cooling system, she mistook the crankcase for the radiator and filled it up! Needless to say, she was perplexed as to why the vehicle didn't make it back out on the road. And when she reported the news to her father, she learned that an overheated radiator isn't the only thing in the world that can give off enormous amounts of steam!

A caution at this point is that anyone looking for a loophole to get out of complying with all that God requires in the area of standards can easily rationalize them away on the basis that times and circumstances have changed. Many violate divine principles under the pretext that we no longer live in the days in which those counsels were written. A familiar saying among us is "Well, that was for their day." While the elapse of time may change how we apply certain counsels, we must be extremely careful how we reason in this matter lest we make "provision for the flesh, to fulfil the lusts thereof" (Rom. 13:14).

## Avoiding Extremes

A safe practice to keep us in the right path is to focus on the standards of God's Word rather than on what society may dictate as acceptable or unacceptable. The world is forever moving away from the will of God while the principles of God, though adaptable, remain intact. "Jesus Christ the same yesterday, and to day, and for ever" (Heb. 13:8). If we are always gauging ourselves by what the world does, we can easily become deceived into thinking that we are staying separate from the world when in truth we are imperceptibly departing from God's standard. Thus the world creeps into us and defiles our religion. It is imperative that we learn to be guided and governed by holy principles instead of following popular fads, movements, and opinions.

However, the opposite course of religious extremism is just as damaging, if not more so. It refuses to acknowledge the role that the world's changing culture has to play in determining how we should carry out biblical principles. Such ideological seeds eventually yield, to varying degrees, a harvest of fanaticism. Fanaticism always brings the church into disrepute with those who would otherwise consider joining it. Only heaven can calculate how many instances misguided religious zeal has injured Christ's cause.

The difficult part is that those who get caught up in such extremes are usually convinced that they are the holiest members of the church. Often they see themselves as part of an elite group that has refused to bow the knee to Baal. Speaking of such a group of fanatics, who attached themselves to his Protestant cause, Martin Luther prayed, "Lord, save me from this church of saints." The Protestant extremists did more to damage Luther's cause than could the pope and all his edicts.

Regrettably, religious extremism will plague the church till the end of time. "As the end draws near, the enemy will work with all his power to bring in fanaticism among us. He would rejoice to see Seventh-day Adventists going to such extremes that they would be branded by the world as a body of fanatics. Against this danger I am bidden to warn ministers and lay members" (GW 316). Our responsibility is to live in a balanced way, avoiding extremes of extravagant worldliness or holiness, both of which will turn people away from us in disgust. Only thus can we get close to the people in order to enlighten their minds about Scripture.

Time will not allow for us to go into detail concerning all the aspects of fanaticism. But in regard to ever-changing lifestyles, both inside as well as outside the church, a safe rule to follow says: "Be not the first by whom the new are tried; nor yet the last to lay the old aside" (Alexander Pope, *An Essay on Criticism*). Thus we shall avoid the new but temporary fads as well as the gazing stock looks clung to from the past. As we learn how to differentiate between the outdated rules of yesteryear and the principles appropriate for our modern age, we shall at the same time discover how to become "all things to all men, that [we] might by all means save some" (1 Cor. 9:22).

It is with a better understanding of how to properly and safely apply divine counsels to our changing times and circumstances that we now consider the lifestyles of the remnant.

## Chapter Five
# Principles of Christian Dress

I t was a busy week as my wife, Lisa, and I prepared for our vacation. We had decided to visit her sister, Judy, in another state. Because my wife and her sister were the only two Adventists out of their large family of eight, it was always a special visit.

Just a few days before our departure, Judy called us. She wanted to know if I would consider speaking to a group of Adventists in her area who had formed a "home church." She said the group felt conditions in the Adventist Church had become too worldly. In reaction, they had decided to pull away from its organized fellowship and had begun worshiping on their own. Judy hoped that some of them would find their way back to the organized church. When she mentioned our planned visit, the group extended me an invitation to conduct their Sabbath morning "home worship service."

Though Judy had briefed us about the group's beliefs, we were still somewhat unprepared for what we met. It conducted its meetings outdoors. Upon arrival we immediately realized we had overdressed for the occasion. Noticing that none of the men wore neckties, I managed to remove mine quickly before we stepped out of the car. But my wife was not so fortunate, because most of the women that morning sported either scarves or bonnets as a covering for their heads.

Now, before you begin to ridicule what we encountered that Sabbath morning, let me say one thing. They turned out to be some of the most sincere people you would ever want to meet. As we became acquainted with them, the Lord impressed me that some of them wanted nothing more than to please Him by doing what they thought He required of them. I could never ridicule anyone for that. As a matter of fact, I have often wished such sincerity was more prevalent in our regular congregations. Though we recognized this group was sincere, at the same time they were sincerely misguided. Their outward appearance evidenced their inner confusion.

As the day wore on, the inevitable took place. During a group discussion the subject of modesty in dress came up. Because it was a favorite topic among them, they did not hesitate to express their convictions. My wife asked them why they felt the need to wear the head covering. As expected, they brought up 1 Corinthians 11, which speaks of a woman needing to cover her head so that she not appear shameful (immodest). I tried to explain to them that the implementation of that particular counsel reflected the circumstances of the time in which Paul wrote it, and therefore no longer applied to our age.

Realizing that to some degree the group viewed us as "worldly Adventists," I figured they regarded my argument as an attempt by the devil to deceive them. It was one of those moments when I was very thankful for more modern inspired counsel to help solve the crisis. Knowing that the group respected the teachings of Ellen White, I found in the home a copy of volume 1 of *Testimonies for the Church*. There, on page 189, I read to them Ellen White's reference to those women in Paul's day: "When they went in public, they covered their faces with a veil." Then speaking of her own day, she added, "In these last days, fashions are shameful and immodest. . . . The small bonnets, exposing the face and head, show a lack of modesty."

The point I made to that group is the same one I wish to establish as we begin this chapter on Christian dress. The principles pertaining to any inspired counsel must be carefully lifted out of the time, place, and circumstances in which it was written and then logically readapted to the modern age to which it is being applied. "Regarding the testimonies, nothing is ignored; nothing is cast aside; but time and place must be considered" (1SM 57).

If this group were trying to follow Paul's counsel to the letter, then their small bonnets and scarves still missed the mark. They would have needed to veil the entire face. (I found very few willing to do that.) Some of them argued that Ellen White was merely calling for only the head to be covered. Indeed she was—back in 1859 when she wrote that counsel. Yet these men and women were even out of harmony with that, because the women were wearing "small" coverings (bonnets and scarves), the very thing she stated to be immodest.

Now the only thing left for them to say was that times had changed since Ellen White had written the statement. "Indeed they have," I agreed. But what they meant by "times have changed" and what I had in mind were two different things. They assumed that their head coverings could now be smaller, whereas I concluded that such things were not necessary at all!

To prove this final point, I referred to the subsequent years of Ellen White's own life, during most of which she wore no head covering at all. Even then one diehard member of the group remarked that Ellen White was not to be our example. Another even suggested that she wore the covering her whole life but that someone had tampered with all the pictures to make it look as though she didn't. At this juncture, as is always the case when people cease to use their common sense, the conversation ceased.

## The History of Dress Reform

To understand how and why the counsel on dress reform initially came to Seventh-day Adventists, we must first reconstruct the times that required it. During the mid 1800s women's fashions consisted of heavy material, and dress lengths were abnormally long, dragging on the sewage-littered ground. Because the skirts hung from the hips, the weight of the fabric pressed on the internal organs. To make matters worse, corsets squeezed the body. It was not uncommon for a corset to reduce a woman's waist size to less than 10 inches in diameter. The effect of clothing on health set the stage for the issue of dress reform to surface, not only in the Adventist Church, but in society itself.

It often comes as a surprise to many Adventists when they learn that the march toward reform in dress began outside the borders of the church. In the 1850s a few nationally prominent women initiated a reform movement to adopt a new style of dress that would avoid such unhealthful practices. The new mode of dress became known as the American costume. It combined a shorter skirt, reaching about halfway from the hip to the knee, with mannish-looking trousers, coat, and vest (see 1T 465; a drawing of some of the new styles appears in George Knight's *Ellen White's World,* p. 38). In 1864 the Lord showed Ellen White that this style of dress was unsuitable for His people.

However, Mrs. White did appeal to Adventist women to adopt a style of dress that addressed health concerns while maintaining modesty. Though the American costume corrected the health problems, adoption of it by Adventists would have injured their witness among unbelievers of that day, since it had become a symbol of the women's rights movement, viewed by most as a radical rebellion against society. Also, many of those associated with the movement were known to be spiritualists. Ellen White warned Adventist women that if they adopted the American costume, their influence would die. "The people would place them on a level with spiritualists and would refuse to listen to them" (1T 457). Consequently, "they would destroy their own influence and that of their husbands. They would become a byword and a derision" (ibid. 422).

Today we might compare this to Adventist believers who would seek to dye their hair green and pierce their tongues. Now, one would be hard pressed to find any health advantages to such bizarre behavior. But back then many were making favorable arguments for the American costume, because it addressed needed reforms in health. Yet Ellen White saw the protection of the Lord's cause from disrepute as of greater importance than even the health benefits it offered. "Some who believe the truth may think that it would be more healthful for the sisters to adopt the American costume, yet if that mode of dress would cripple our influence among unbelievers so that we could not so readily gain access to them, we should by no means adopt it, though we suffered much in consequence [in health]" (ibid. 456, 457). So it should be for us today as we try to relate to lifestyle choices. We should always have foremost in our minds as to the kind of influence our decisions will have on the cause of Christ in the area where we live.

The dilemma between healthful dress and a healthful witness became a real concern to many Adventist leaders in the mid 1860s. In response Ellen White wrote and published an article in 1867 entitled "Reform in Dress" (see 1T 456-466). In it she recommended a general pattern that embodied principles intended to solve the crisis. However, contrary to the belief of many even today, the Lord revealed no particular dress style or pattern. Referring to that pattern in later years, Mrs. White wrote, "Some have supposed that the very pattern given [in 1867] was the pattern that all were to adopt. This is not so. . . . No one precise style has been given me as the exact rule to guide all in their dress" (letter 19, 1897; in 1T 718).

The years following the mid-nineteenth century saw the general styles of women's dress change for the better, becoming more sensible and healthful. The need for the old dress reform pattern ceased. Yet Ellen White continued to promote the fundamental principles revealed by God to guide the Christian in this area of lifestyle practice.

Let us now take a closer look at these principles and seek a balanced application of them in our more modern day.

## Health Factors

Health principles are important. Though Ellen White counseled early Adventists to avoid inappropriate styles even though they offered some healthful benefits to them, the counsel did move the church to adopt a more acceptable style that corrected the health concerns. Still, even today, the need to preserve one's health should play a big part in determining how we dress. We can be thankful that although some health-destroying fashions still exist, God's people have a wide variety of choices that offer freedom from any really serious health consequences.

We should wear nothing that will seriously restrict the function of the internal organs or the flow of blood to all parts of our body. The human anatomy has not changed over time. Nor has the way in which our blood circulates. Good circulation is vital to general health and longevity. Especially in cold weather, women as well as men should seek to clothe their bodies, particularly their extremities, so as to avoid chill. Pants, or slacks, offer women some real benefit in this area (see 1T 461).

However, while some elect to wear pants underneath a skirt or dress, others have chosen to wear them alone. While either mode solves the health problem, the wearing of pants by women has from time to time caused controversy in our standard-oriented church. Some more conservative minds object to pants for women, claiming that they violate Scripture. They quote Deuteronomy 22:5: "The woman shall not wear that which pertaineth unto a man, neither shall a man put on a woman's garment: for all that do so are abomination to the Lord thy God." Commenting on this verse, Ellen White wrote: "There is an increasing tendency to have women in their dress and appearance as near like the other sex as possible, and to fashion their dress very much like that of men, but God pronounces it abomination" (*ibid.* 421).

## In Accordance With the Bible

Here we have come to another important principle for the Christian—that we have a biblical reason for what we do. This principle should pertain not only to what we wear, but whatever else we choose to make a part of our life practice. If we are truly Christ's representatives here on earth, then shouldn't we seek to follow the guidelines He laid down for us?

I have a burden that we know for sure that whatever we seek to promote by our example truly does have a sound biblical argument in its defense. If it doesn't, then we simply come across to people as fanatical or bigoted in our opinions. And of course, sound biblical arguments must stem from Scripture itself and not from our own private interpretation. For example, let's explore further whether Deuteronomy 22:5 forbids women wearing pants. The passage asks that men and women dress in a manner that clearly distinguishes the genders—a relevant counsel for our age of unisex! But let's go back to the days of ancient Israel, the people for whom this counsel first applied, and investigate the style of dress they themselves wore.

In biblical times neither men nor women wore pants or slacks. In fact, in those days men and women dressed very much alike. Genesis 37:3 says that Jacob made Joseph "a long robe with sleeves" (RSV). Second Samuel 13:18 states that Tamar, the daughter of David, wore "a long robe with sleeves" (RSV). The Hebrew word describing this "long robe with sleeves" is the same in both passages.

We can only conclude that in biblical times men and women dressed very much alike—*but not completely.* According to Isaiah 3:16-23, the "daughters of Zion" were distinguished from the men by their various articles of jewelry and veils. But most Adventist women today wear neither jewelry nor veils. No, but certain styles of clothes, even pants, distinctly identify the gender (that's why a normal man doesn't go to a women's clothing store to shop for himself).

In all fairness to biblical exegesis, one can only conclude that

Deuteronomy 22:5 is simply saying that it is God's desire that we make enough distinction in dress so that others will never mistake men for women or women for men. A. W. Spalding observed that "this law [Deuteronomy 22:5] struck at the practice of transvestism, the interchange of dress of the sexes for the purpose of cross-sexual expression, involving homosexuality" (*Captains of the Host,* vol. 1, p. 344). Ellen White seemed to indicate the same when she stated that "the same dress worn by both sexes would cause confusion and great increase of crime" (1 T 460).

As we have seen, to automatically condemn all pants worn by women on the basis of Scripture lacks scriptural support. It is merely one's personal interpretation of the Scripture. Nor can one build a solid case against it from the writings of Ellen White when we take those counsels in their context of time and circumstances. Robert Olson, former secretary of the Ellen G. White Estate, offers us his conclusion: "In light of Ellen White's counsels, what attitude should Adventist women take toward the wearing of slacks? It hardly seems justifiable to conclude that Mrs. White's writings stand in opposition to the wearing of all pants or slacks by women. However, if Mrs. White were living today, she would no doubt take exception to the wearing by women of tight-fitting clothing of any kind, whether slacks, sweaters, or skirts. She would also most likely have something uncomplimentary to say about the wearing of short skirts. But, in the opinion of many, she would not protest against the wearing of those truly modest slacks or pantsuits which make it possible for the wearer to retain a distinctive feminine appearance" ("Can Christian Women Wear Slacks?" chapel talk at Pacific Union College, Mar. 6, 1974).

Once again, my burden is not to promote the wearing of any certain style of dress, but rather to help us be sure we are on proper scriptural footing as we try to give reasons for what we do. Returning to the women who wore the head coverings that day, my struggle with them was not so much over the fact that they were wearing a covering. If that is what they felt comfortable doing, who am I to ridicule or condemn it? Christians of other faiths, such as the Amish, Mennonites, Brethren, and old school Pentecostals do the same. My only concern was that some of them were attempting to use Scripture as a reason they—and in their opinion, everyone—should be doing it.

I know an Adventist woman who I think has a healthy Christian attitude toward the principle of this whole matter. She made a decision nearly 15 years ago to stop wearing pants or slacks. Since that time she has never gone out in public wearing anything but a dress or skirt. When I asked her why she did this she told me that such apparel makes her feel more ladylike. Upon further inquiry I discovered that she had become settled in her convictions but in no way sought to apply her way of dressing as a criterion for anyone else. In fact, she told me that some of her closest friends wore pants on a regular basis. Would that all of us in the church possess such spiritual maturity. We should never ostracize such individuals in any way because they don't dress like the crowd and choose not to wear pants like most women in the church today do.

And neither should people more conservative in their dress try to decide for those who adopt the more modern forms of dress. Such may feel justified in their opinion on the basis of what they mistakenly think is biblical, but they will inevitably end up where they don't belong—usurping God's judgment throne.

Such individuals need to be more worried about reforming their own attitudes than they do other people's dress. But God loves them, too, and has given relevant counsel to help them. "Talk of the love and humility of Jesus, but do not encourage the brethren and sisters to engage in picking flaws in the dress or appearance of one another. Some take delight in this work; and when their minds are turned this direction, they begin to feel that they must become church tinkers. They climb upon the judgment seat, and as soon as they see one of their brethren and sisters, they look to find something to criticize. This is one of the most effectual means of becoming narrow-minded and of dwarfing spiritual growth. God would have them step down from the judgment seat, for He has never placed them there" (CG 429).

## Modesty

The love of dress endangers the morals and makes the woman the opposite of the Christian lady characterized by modesty and sobriety. Showy, extravagant dress too often encourages lust in the heart of the wearer and awakens base passions in the heart of the beholder" (4T 645). Besides the words we speak, few things reveal what is really in the human heart more than outward dress. Fashion has always served as one of society's strongest statements of human pride and means of self-promotion. And today Ellen White's counsel applies to males as well as females.

The Bible clearly teaches that modesty should be one of the primary principles used in guiding the Christian to dress appropriately. "In like manner also, that women adorn themselves in modest apparel" (1 Tim. 2:9).

Rarely do we fully define or comprehend the term *modesty*. Many think that it pertains to inappropriate dress from a sexual perspective. Certainly this aspect of dress—or maybe in this case, the lack of it—has a valid application. In the book *Seventh-day Adventists Believe* we find this statement regarding our denominational stand on the relation of dress to morality: "Christians will not mar the beauty of their characters with styles that arouse the 'lust of the flesh' (1 John 2:16). Because they want to witness to others, they will dress and act modestly, *not accentuating the parts of the body that stimulate sexual desires.* Modesty promotes moral health. The Christian's aim is to glorify God, not self" (p. 286; italics supplied).

To dress in a way that we know will stimulate others sexually promotes sensuality that can more easily lead to fornication and adultery. Though these sins have become somewhat socially acceptable by our world today, for the true Christian they are as abhorrent as they were when the Lord sent the prophet Nathan to confront King David on the subject (see 2 Sam. 12). We must be careful here. If we dress for the purpose of sexual arousal, our motives render us guilty of such serious sins even though we may not actually commit the act.

However, the putting on of more clothing doesn't cure the carnal nature. Even in cultures in which people have taken pains to "overdress," they can still become victimized by eroticism. I have personally observed this in some ultraconservative areas. Despite the severity of dress, such environments often reek with an unhealthful amount of sexual energy seething just beneath the surface, ready to break out at any moment of weakness. In an environment in which women always wear their hair up in a bun, even something as simple as the "letting down of the hair" can have sensual overtones.

Now, I'm not suggesting that Adventists wear less clothing. What I'm trying to bring out is that the counsel regarding "modesty" is broader than one might initially think. Webster's defines *modest* as: "(1) disliking praise, publicity, etc.; (2) avoiding self-exposure; (3) not outstanding." Here is the concept of modesty at its best, as we seek to avoid directing attention to ourselves. We can violate the principle as much through extremely conservative styles of dress as by greater exposure of the body. Adventists have always had a class who, while they condemn others for immodest dress, actually carry out a form of immodesty of their own. They "take pains to make themselves gazing-stocks by dressing differently from the world," something Ellen White advised us not to do (2SM 476).

Modesty is a relative term. What is modest in one age of the world or culture may not be so in another. That's what I was trying desperately to explain that day to the people wearing the head coverings. In the early 1850s Ellen White taught that "small bonnets" were immodest. Do we really believe that she would advocate the same in our present society? It would have been immodest for Jesus to have dressed like a twenty-first-century American male. Likewise, it would be just as immodest for one today to go around wearing the same clothing as Jesus wore.

As seen in the example of the American costume, what society considered acceptable played a real part in determining just how our people back then were to dress. Once again, it involves the fact that it does matter to the Lord how unbelievers view us. To remain modest we must adopt "a style of dress appropriate for the age" in which we live (*Story of Our Health Message*, p. 146). Also, modesty demands that the dress be appropriate not only for the age in which we live, but for the age of the person wearing it as well. Here we get back to the matter of taste. The clothing that a teenage girl wears most often does not look good on an older woman. Likewise, a 15-year-old girl dressing like a 50-year-old woman would tend to draw attention to herself.

This is also true for varying cultures. Tropical island wear is certainly out of place during Minnesota's winter months, just as the wearing of long johns on the beach would create gossip in tropical regions. We need to avoid, as far as possible, making ourselves a subject of controversy, a principle in harmony with avoiding publicity through self-exposure. Notice that "we are not to feel it our duty to wear a pilgrim's dress of just such a color, just such a shape, but neat, modest apparel, that the word of inspiration teaches us we should wear. . . . *Nothing will be put upon the person to attract attention or to create controversy*" (TM 130, 131).

Here we see that modesty also calls for our clothing to be neat. Modest dress excludes the wearing of sloppy, untasteful clothing. God also saw need to lead His messenger to instruct us upon this point: "Another class who lacked taste and order in dress have taken advantage of what I have written [concerning pride of dress] and have gone to the opposite extreme; considering that they were free from pride, they have looked upon those who dress neatly and orderly as being proud. Oddity and carelessness in dress have been considered a special virtue by some. Such take a course which destroys their influence over unbelievers. They disgust those whom they might benefit" (1T 275).

Right principles in dress will never excuse cheap, unattractive clothing. To purchase clothing made of durable, quality clothing that is well fitting, tasteful, and long lasting does not indicate pride, but good common sense. It is also many times a wise financial investment because of its long-lasting quality. Jesus followed this principle. He wore a robe of such high quality that even Roman soldiers gambled for it. The prudent shopper knows how to find such quality wear at affordable prices.

## Extremes in Dress

Seventh-day Adventists seek to lift up to the world the beauty of obeying the Lord's will in all areas of life. Because of this we as a denomination have been and still are vulnerable to "a conscientiousness that will carry everything to extremes, and make Christian duties [such as dress reform] as burdensome as the Jews made the observance of the Sabbath" (2SM 319). A good precaution to follow is to "Be very cautious not to advance too fast, lest we be obliged to retrace our steps. *In reforms we would better come one step short of the mark than to go one step beyond it*. And if there is error at all, let it be on the side next to the people [who are following the present norms]" (3T 21; italics supplied). This is vitally necessary so "our dress may commend itself to the judgment of candid minds" (2T 66; see also p. 378).

Our past history painfully reminds us that while dress reform can greatly bless God's people and their witness, Satan can turn it into a curse by leading members to go to extremes with it. While some have ignored the subject altogether, thinking it nonessential, others have made it one of the central themes of their religion. But Jesus said: "Do not be worried about your life, as to what you will eat or what you will drink; nor for your body, as to what you will put on. Is not life more than food, and the body more than clothing? . . . And why are you worried about clothing? Observe how the lilies of the field grow; they do not toil nor do they spin, yet I say to you that not even Solomon in all his glory clothed himself like one of these. But if God so clothes the grass of the field, which is alive today and tomorrow is thrown into the furnace, will He not much more clothe you? You of little faith! Do not worry then, saying, 'What will we eat?' or 'What will we drink?' or 'What will we wear for clothing?' For the Gentiles eagerly seek all these things" (Matt. 6:25-32, NASB).

Ellen White once again put it all in perspective when she counseled us to use common sense in carrying out these principles and then "let not the dress question fill the mind" (CG 414). She considered it as one of the "minor things" that "never should have been urged as a testing truth necessary to salvation" (RH, Oct. 8, 1867).

## A Test Question?

To some in Ellen White's day the issue of dress reform was a scary one. They feared that the Lord was trying to use it to make them look weird in the sight of their family, friends, and neighbors. But Ellen White consoled them: "None need fear that I shall make dress reform one of my principal subjects as we travel from place to place" (1T 523).

Here we catch a glimpse of the balance Mrs. White herself had on the subject. She did not intend for the dress issue to serve as a test. But her position upset another class who felt strongly that God's people needed to dress a certain way in order to be assured of their right standing with Him. Referring to this mind-set, she wrote: "Some were greatly troubled because I did not make the dress [the reform dress of 1867] a test question, and still others because I advised those who had unbelieving husbands or children not to adopt the reform dress, as it might lead to unhappiness that would counteract all the good to be derived from its use" (4T 637). God was and still is more interested in the unity and happiness of a family than He is over what they wear. Contrary to what some may think, the Lord is still dynamic in His ability to meet and work with people where they are in the context of their little earthly lives. He wants lifestyle reforms implemented on the basis of how they will effect one's witness to the greater testing truths (righteousness by faith, the Sabbath, etc). To be a positive witness, we are to advance in areas of lifestyle gradually and sensibly as God opens the way for it.

The early Christian church had to work through similar situations. For example, take the issue over circumcision. Many felt that it was absolutely necessary for people to be circumcised in order to join the church and be saved. They appealed to the writings of the prophet Moses as proof for their position. Local churches hotly debated the issue, and it finally ended up on the agenda for the General Conference session in Jerusalem (see Acts 15). At that session the notorious Paul, a delegate for the Gentile churches, argued as he always did that "circumcision is nothing, and uncircumcision is nothing, *but the keeping of the commandments of God"* (1 Cor. 7:19). In other words, from the perspective of salvation and church membership circumcision was a nontesting issue. Unlike many in his day, Paul considered Moses' writing on the subject as no longer applicable because of changed circumstances. To Paul, the keeping of the commandments were the real "testing truths."

Once the church accepted the fact that uncircumcised Gentiles were as saved as circumcised Jews, it took the teeth out of the over-conscientious Jews' bite as they tried to rein in other consciences according to their own. It sent everyone back to their own corner to focus on the real reasons for their own choices. Also it helped make more winsome Christians, as we see evidenced in Peter's experience of coming to accept the Gentile converts where they were (see Acts 10, 11). Becoming a more effective element in God's cause, he now could join Paul in allowing God to use him to be "all things to all men" (1 Cor. 9:22). And for what purpose? That he "might by all means save some."

Though we can accept the fact that Paul was correct in treating certain counsels of Moses as being outdated, we have a tough time admitting that the same might hold true for some of the things Ellen White wrote. Especially is this the case as one tries to apply things written in an age of Puritanism to our modern society.

What's more, we seem afraid to accept people as worthy of our fellowship unless they come up to certain lifestyle marks to which we think we have already risen. We preach the gospel to them, and when they respond with a desire to be baptized, we lay out a list of lifestyle measures they must attain to in order to be worthy of baptism. Thus we tend to create legalists right up front by giving them the message that they must become better before they can have the assurance of a walk with Christ. I always thought baptism was just a public statement that people desire to die to self and live for Christ. If they have stepped out to keep God's commandments, especially in making a stand for the Sabbath, why do we then hang them up on stringent details concerning lifestyle? "Because its evidence that they aren't completely dead to self yet," someone replies. Well, I ask, who is? Baptism marks only the beginning of the dying process that continues for the rest of our earthly life.

Of course, ministers should always remember that it is their duty before God to enlighten new believers on certain lifestyle issues. I'm not talking about lowering the standard. I certainly never would advocate baptism of anyone who does not show a genuine desire to change. But some of the things we associate their church membership with are nothing more than human-made roadblocks.

For example, many ministers require a baptismal candidate to gain absolute, complete victory over smoking before they will baptize them into church membership.

I personally know of a case in which a woman who had been drinking liquor and smoking three packs of cigarettes a day for 30 years attended a series of Adventist evangelistic meetings. Within the first three weeks she accepted Jesus Christ as her Lord and Saviour, began observing the biblical Sabbath, fervently believed all the other doctrinal concepts that she had heard presented, quit drinking alcohol, and made the decision to move out from a live-in situation she had with a man she was not married to. At the end of the five-week campaign she was so happy in Jesus! One couldn't help noticing in her expression the change that had taken place in her heart. She desired nothing more than to be baptized into Christ and join His church. Then the pastor asked how her struggle with smoking was going. She responded that she had smoked only two cigarettes during the last 10 days of the meetings (compare that to 60 cigarettes per day for the past 30 years). At that point he deferred her baptism until she got "total victory."

Ellen White gave the church some biblical counsel regarding smoking as it relates to church membership: "The unreasonable, unchristian course of men and women who had more zeal than knowledge or piety, has displeased and dishonored God. He calls upon them to repent. Some have taken the position that those who use tobacco should be dealt with and turned out of the church at once; but with some who would engage in this work there are greater defilements of the soul-temple than tobacco can make. *In all our experience for many years, not a case of this kind has been thus treated.* We have borne for years with those in the slavery of habit, and unless there was some other cause for such action, we have not felt at liberty to deal with them or separate them from the church. We have prayed and labored with them, and in many cases have after a time succeeded in winning them fully. Those who did not reform, became lax in other things, and *gave up their efforts to overcome,* so that offenses of a grievous character occurred that required action on the part of the church" (15MR 139; italics supplied).

Notice she focuses here on "their efforts to overcome." I certainly would never advocate baptism for anyone who has not indicated a real conviction to overcome a habit such as smoking. But 1 John 1:9 says that *"if we confess our sins,* he is faithful and just to forgive us our sins, and to cleanse us from all unrighteousness." Notice it does not say "If we overcome our sins, he is faithful and just to forgive us our sins." In the eyes of God confessing that something is sinful is the real essence of overcoming it. And if God considers such individuals as "cleansed" the moment they confess, who are we to treat them as though they are still defiled by forbidding them the water of baptism? (See again Acts 10 and 11.)

Ultimately it should boil down to a judgment call on the part of the pastor as it pertains to the individual circumstances of the one under consideration for baptism. Compassionate pastors will base their decisions to baptize more on the candidate's desire to change rather than requiring total victory. What's more, they will see to it that they get their churches involved in doing whatever they can to help and encourage the one who has already overcome spiritually to make that decision a reality in the flesh! Ultimately, a lot of the responsibility falls upon the pastor and church members who are to be their "brother's keeper."

Now, I know that many will object to such a suggestion. We have it inbred in us to think that giving people Christian acceptance before they really come up to our standards will eventually lead to the church's demise. Sure, if we follow the approach I suggested we may get a few more smokers in the church, but if God took care of the church back then, He will take care of it today. Our job as church members is to be meeting people's needs, both within the church and without, at the level where they are hurting. Never should we make "tests" out of issues that God never intended.

## Love Is the Answer

The bottom line is that Adventists have never needed prelates to tell them exactly what they should or shouldn't wear. Ellen White, though faithful in laying out principles on the subject, refused to dictate fashion. She knew that if the heart was not fully surrendered to Jesus, it was futile to try to deal with outward adornment. "Cleanse the fountain," she wrote, "and the streams will be pure. If the heart is right, your words, your dress, your acts will all be right" (1T 158). People who are in love with Jesus will be just as cooperative in letting Him clothe them according to His splendor as are the lilies of the field.

I remember when I fell in love with the young woman who would become my wife. One day after we had dated for several months she was unusually quiet. Detecting that something was troubling her, I asked what was wrong. Embarrassed, she said she had for a while been wanting to tell me something but was afraid it would hurt my feelings. I assured her that unless she planned to break off our relationship, nothing she could say would hurt my feelings. With a deep sigh, she proceeded to inform me that she didn't like the way I dressed. My background was that of a farmer. I guess she felt I needed to reform my taste in clothing (she had come from a more cultured environment).

Now, I could have gotten offended and stubbornly reacted by saying that what she saw was what she got, take it or leave it, but I didn't. No, my immediate response was "Well, honey, don't you worry about it. I'll start wearing whatever you want me to. As a matter of fact, I've got an extra $1,000, so tomorrow let's just go down to Atlanta and let you pick out some new clothes for me." And that is exactly what we did. From that point on my outward appearance drastically changed (and so did my bank account!). But it didn't matter to me. I did it all with indescribable joy in my heart!

The following weekend I was back in my hometown among some of my friends. When I walked into the room they began whistling and joking about the new me. "What happened to you, Hayden?" My answer was easy. "Boys, *I'm in looooove!*"

This brings us back around to the real question, which is: Have we fallen in love with Jesus to the point at which we will enthusiastically order our lives in such a way so as to please Him? The apostle Paul said that those who have, will naturally "always be trying to find out what best pleases the Lord" (Eph. 5:10, TCNT). Once we fall in love with Jesus our desire to please God resolves the problem of needed reforms. But if people have not given their hearts to Christ, then urging such issues as dress reform will only push them further away from God and the church. "There is no use in telling you that you must not wear this or that, for if the love of these vain things is in your heart, your laying off your adornments will only be like cutting the foliage off a tree. The inclinations of the natural heart would again assert themselves. You must have a conscience of your own" (SD 292).

Ellen White tells us that sanctification is a progressive process that will continue as long as life shall last (SL 94, 10). We need to realize that love for Jesus takes time to grow in the natural heart. We cannot expect people to overcome everything all at once, or even in five weeks of meetings. Evangelistic workers need to look more for a change in the heart instead of perfection in the flesh. "Man looketh on the outward appearance, but the Lord looketh on the heart" (1 Sam. 16:7). If God operates on this principle, shouldn't we follow it in our evangelism?

"There is a medium position [balance] in these things [regarding what is appropriate to wear]. Oh, that all might wisely find that position and keep it. In this solemn time let us all search our own hearts, repent of our sins, and humble ourselves before God. The work is between God and our own souls. It is an individual work, and all will have enough to do without criticizing the dress, actions, and motives of their brethren and sisters" (1T 425, 426).

Here is where the entire dress question, as well as most other lifestyle-related issues, should be settled—by the individual conscience. We need to be careful, lest thinking we are God's appointed standard keepers, we trample upon the consciences of others. "Some who adopted the [dress] reform were not content to show by example the advantages of the dress, giving, *when asked,* their reasons for adopting it, and letting the matter rest there. They sought to control others' conscience by their own. If they wore it, others must put it on. They forgot that none were compelled to wear the reform dress. It was not my duty to urge the subject upon my sisters. After presenting it before them as it had been shown me, I left them to their own conscience" (4T 636; italics supplied).

Of course, it should be understood that most of the counsel regarding dress pertains to individual church members. It does not necessarily apply to the running of institutions such as schools, hospitals, or other businesses in which there might be advantages to having a dress code. Administrators of such institutions should have the right and responsibility to set some limits on standards. Even McDonald's recognizes the advantages of having its employees uphold certain dress codes.

Also, the church in general must be careful to maintain a certain degree of standards among its members, lest we lose our capacity to witness. I am not advocating a free-for-all. God did not design standards just for the protection of individuals, but for the church's corporate reputation as well. When members become totally oblivious to sound reason and treat the subject as though there are no limitations, then the leaders of the church must bring things back to order. Though we must be careful not to let things get out of hand, we are never to react to something too quickly just because it is not traditional, lest we wound a person for whom Christ died.

Those who earnestly desire to be fitting representatives for Jesus on earth will prayerfully take the matter of Christian dress before the

Lord to discover their individual duty. If we would only go alone before a mirror and honestly ask ourselves, "Does my apparel glorify God, or is it designed to call undue attention to myself? How does my dress affect my ability to relate to those around me whom I desire to reach for the Lord?" it would solve most difficulties regarding the subject. Those who are honest in their self-evaluation will have their answer, because the Holy Spirit has promised to be our guide.

*Chapter Six*
# Principles of Adornment

We have now in our study reached what I believe has become one of the most hotly debated issues in the Adventist Church: What does the Bible say about the wearing of jewelry? The church has a long history of maintaining that the Word of God condemns jewelry, but is that really the case? Or are our antijewelry views derived more from concepts that have just become tradition in our church over time? In this chapter we shall attempt to answer some of these questions.

I have carefully listened to the arguments of many pastors and evangelists about what the Bible teaches concerning jewelry and other ornaments. Once again, my research examined a fairly wide spectrum of views ranging from staunchly conservative to a more liberal accommodation of the subject. Taking each into consideration, I have spent many hours in the Bible attempting to draw my own personal conclusion as to how I should relate to the issue. What I have found, I would now like to share.

## *The Idolatry of Jewels*

In Genesis 35 the patriarch Jacob prepared his extended household to go before the Lord in worship. He told them to "put away the strange gods that are among you," and "they gave unto Jacob all the strange gods which were in their hand, and all their earrings which were in their ears; and Jacob hid them under the oak tree which was by Shechem" (Gen. 35:2, 4).

Years later the household of Israel (Jacob) returned to the Promised Land during their exodus from Egyptian bondage. While their leader Moses was on an extended visit to the mountain of God, the people grew impatient and made a cult image in the form of a golden calf (Ex. 32:1-4). Commenting on the incident, the book of Acts says that when the people bowed before the golden calf they worshiped "the host of heaven" (see Acts 7:40-42). How could they have been worshiping the "host of heaven"—the sun, moon, and stars—through the golden calf? The answer lies in the material they used to make the idolatrous calf. They fashioned the golden calf from the gold earrings the people had brought with them out of Egypt (see Ex. 32:1-4).

Many have used these two accounts in an attempt to prove that the Bible considers the wearing of jewelry idolatrous. At first glance it appears valid. But a hidden aspect of the texts makes the condemnation of all jewelry as idolatry not as cut-and-dried as we might like. The earrings that Jacob's household wore they had bought from their surrounding pagan culture. Likewise, the earrings melted down for the golden calf came from the Egyptians. Ancient Near Eastern peoples engraved the images of their gods onto their ornaments. This of course violated the second commandment.

Archaeological digs have uncovered such engraved trinkets. What made the jewelry idolatrous was the images on them. "In the Bible, earrings were often associated with idolatry. Jacob asked his family to stop their idolatry, and give up their earrings, which he buried (Genesis 35:4). The prophet Hosea associated the wearing of jewelry with the worship of Baal (Hosea 2:13, 17). *Earrings became connected with idolatry because heathen nations engraved strange deities and figures on their earrings and other jewelry.* This was thought to ward off evil and bring good fortune to a family. They were like good luck charms, except they were taken much more seriously" (*The Victor Handbook of Bible Knowledge,* p. 69; italics supplied).

"In the superstitious Near Eastern nations many people feared imaginary spirits. To protect themselves, they wore magical charms. The amulets referred to in the Bible were earrings worn by women (Genesis 35:4; Judges 2:13; 8:24), or pendants suspended from the chains around the necks of men. *The amulet had sacred words or the figure of a god engraved on it. . . .* Women also wore amulets to insure fertility. Jeremiah the prophet noted another common heathen practice: The women of Judah kneaded cakes, gave drink offerings, and burned incense to the 'queen of heaven' to assure fertility (Jeremiah 44:17-19; cf. 7:18). The 'queen' mentioned in this passage was probably Astarte (Ashtoreth), the Canaanite goddess of sexual love, maternity, and fertility. Of course, all of these superstitious practices were evil in God's sight" (*Illustrated Manners and Customs of the Bible,* pp. 442, 481; italics supplied).

The Bible itself contains several references to the practice of turning ornaments into idols by either engraving the images of gods upon them or using the material to form an idolatrous image (see Eze. 7:20; 16:17; Isa. 30:22). The point I want to make here is that we cannot justly condemn jewelry as idolatry by these texts unless the ornaments bear graven images or are used in a superstitious or otherwise idolatrous way.

For example, when my wife was a little girl she and her family were caught in a frightening electrical storm. In her fear she felt comfort in that she was wearing her scapular, a small piece of fabric representing a sleeveless religious garment. She had been taught that wearing it would not only constantly remind her of her commitment to God, but also invoke the intercession of the blessed mother and thus bring blessings to her life. Many feel that by wearing a cross they are somehow closer to God and have a better guarantee of safety and good fortune. Such ornaments become objects of idolatry because they subtly replace a person's direct trust in God.

However, the broader principle of truth we need to learn here is that it doesn't necessarily have to be an ornament to be idolatrous. Anything we place reliance on instead of total trust in the mighty God of heaven becomes an object of idolatry. Many, even among Adventists who would condemn all jewelry as idolatry, rely more upon their financial wealth to get them through certain hardships than they do God. What is it that makes the driving of a prestigious car sometimes respectable while we would condemn a young woman for her $10 pair of earrings? Cannot such be as equally idolatrous in God's sight?

## God's Promotion of Jewelry

It may shock many, as it did me, to discover that the Bible reveals God as a promoter of fine jewelry. Now, before any declare me a heretic and prepare the kindling to burn me at the stake for making such a statement, at least hear me out. We may have our pet ideas about a subject, but the truth is that when we come to the Bible on any given topic we must let the weight of Bible evidence determine our conclusions. The truly wise will acknowledge the truth of what Scripture states, even if it upsets the applecart of traditional thinking.

Adventists often chastise other Christians regarding the way they use certain scriptures to support traditional errors, such as the immortality of the soul or the wrong worship day. Such individuals take an à la carte approach to the Bible by choosing those texts that appear to prove their point while ignoring other passages that challenge their cherished conclusion. Yet we Adventists have done the exact same thing when it comes to issues such as the wearing of jewelry. We like to quote certain texts that by themselves make it appear that God is totally antijewelry, but leave off those equally inspired statements indicating that God is not as adamant against such things as we try to make Him out to be.

Check it out in your concordance. For every text in the Bible that speaks of ornaments negatively you will find two or three in which God speaks of them favorably. For our first parents' enjoyment the Lord furnished them a land (Havilah) enriched with gold, pearls (bdellium), and onyx (Gen. 2:10-12). The Lord instructed the high priest of the sanctuary service to wear gold and precious stones (Ex. 28). God created Lucifer with a covering of gold and precious stones, and he even walked on "stones of fire" in the Most Holy Place. In all this God considered him as being "perfect in beauty" and "perfect in [his] ways" (see Eze. 28:12-15). Even Jesus, our Lord and Saviour, will wear a "golden crown" on His head when He returns to earth for us, at which time He will also present us with one (Rev. 14:14; 2 Tim. 4:8).

But for more thorough observation of how the Bible presents God's attitude toward jewelry, let's explore a text in Isaiah. Because of Israel's infidelity God spoke to them through His prophet. "Moreover the Lord saith, Because the daughters of Zion are haughty, and walk with stretched forth necks and wanton eyes, walking and mincing as they go, and making a tinkling with their feet: Therefore the Lord will smite with a scab the crown of the head of the daughters of Zion, and the Lord will discover their secret parts. In that day the Lord will take away the bravery of their tinkling ornaments about their feet, and their cauls, and their round tires like the moon, the chains, and the bracelets, and the mufflers, the bonnets, and the ornaments of the legs, and the headbands, and the tablets, and the earrings, the rings, and nose jewels, the changeable suits of apparel, and the mantles, and the wimples, and the crisping pins, the glasses, and the fine linen, and the hoods, and the vails. And it shall come to pass, that instead of sweet smell there shall be stink; and instead of a girdle a rent; and instead of well set hair baldness; and instead of a stomacher a girding of sackcloth; and burning instead of beauty" (Isa. 3:16-24).

Bible scholars would tell us that there are two ways of extracting the full meaning of this passage. First, the context is literal in that Isaiah's day found the women of Israel frequenting the shops of the Phonecian craftsmen to buy their ornaments and clothes. Once again, these articles most often bore the engravings of the Phoenician gods.

The second application is that the items Isaiah condemned indicated a much deeper problem—Israel's spiritual condition. God had taken the Hebrews, one of the most lowly and insignificant nations of the earth, and had used them to demonstrate His power to reform. Now His people had turned away from Him. The jewelry in this case symbolized Israel's apostasy. A similar correlation between the misuse of jewelry and idolatry appears in Hosea 2:13.

Now for the purpose of our inquiry, can we really use these texts in a way to prove that God is altogether against jewelry? To answer that question let us go to Ezekiel 16. It reveals how Israel initially received those ornaments that she corrupted with paganism. In the first eight verses of this chapter we find an account of how God found Israel destitute of any real earthly value and through a "covenant" with her "caused thee [Israel] to multiply as the bud of the field, and thou hast increased and waxen great, *and thou art come to excellent ornaments: thy breasts are fashioned, and thine hair is grown, whereas thou wast naked and bare*" (Eze. 16:7).

Now, notice what God reminds Israel He did for her when He made her His. "Then washed I thee with water; yea, I thoroughly washed away thy blood from thee, and I anointed thee with oil. I clothed thee also with broidered work, and shod thee with badgers' skin, and I girded thee about with fine linen, and I covered thee with silk. *I decked thee also with ornaments, and I put bracelets upon thy hands, and a chain on thy neck. And I put a jewel on thy forehead, and earrings in thine ears, and a beautiful crown upon thine head. Thus wast thou decked with gold and silver;* and thy raiment was of fine linen, and silk, and broidered work; thou didst eat fine flour, and honey, and oil: and thou wast exceeding beautiful, and thou didst prosper into a kingdom. And thy renown went forth among the heathen for thy beauty: for it was perfect through my comeliness, which I had put upon thee, saith the Lord God" (verses 9-14).

Here we see clearly that it was God who symbolically decked out His bride Israel. Does this sound as though He arbitrarily forbids jewelry? Hardly! In fact, after He dressed her up in fine clothes and jewels and stood back and looked at her, He declared that she was "exceeding beautiful" (verse 13).

In this context God does not consider these ornamental tokens of love as idolatrous but rather as symbols of His own righteousness that He covered her with. We see the same symbolism even more strongly in Isaiah 61:10: "I will greatly rejoice in the Lord, my soul shall be joyful in my God; for he hath clothed me with the garments of salvation, he hath covered me with the robe of righteousness, *as a bridegroom decketh himself with ornaments, and as a bride adorneth herself with her jewels."*

The passage reminds me of another portion of Scripture in which God adorned His bride. "And I John saw the holy city, new Jerusalem, coming down from God out of heaven, prepared as a bride adorned for her husband" (Rev. 21:2). As I studied this it was as though God invited me to look at His wedding album. God told me to "come hither, I will shew thee the bride, the Lamb's wife. . . . And he . . . shewed me that great city, the holy Jerusalem, descending out of heaven from God, having the glory of God" (verses 9-11).

What I saw was most surprising. I had often used as an argument for God's condemnation of jewelry the fact that another great city spoken of in Revelation 17, also known as the "great whore," was decked out "with gold and precious stones and pearls" (Rev. 17:4). You can imagine my surprise as I peered into God's wedding photos of Revelation 21 and saw Him proudly standing next to His bride, who was adorned with the very same articles: gold (Rev. 21:18 and 21), precious stones (verses 11, 18-20), and a string of pearls around her neck of walls (verse 21).

We even try to contrast the harlot's outward adorning, as described in Revelation 17:4, with that of another woman whom God obviously acknowledges as His: "a woman clothed with the sun, and the moon under her feet" (Rev. 12:1). But even here our argument breaks down when we read that she has "upon her head a crown of twelve stars."

Needless to say, many of the traditional arguments we employ against jewelry, such as the one involving the harlot of Revelation 17, are flimsy. But that is always the case when we refuse to deal squarely with what Scripture really has to say about a given topic. Because of our dishonesty with Scripture, we damage our credibility in the eyes of real biblical thinkers and obscure the great principles of the Word, which are in fact the best argument against decorating the human body with jewels. (We shall deal with these great principles later in this chapter.)

To return to Ezekiel 16, after the Lord did so much for Israel and adorned her in His glorious fashion, she played the harlot. As with Lucifer, whom God had created with a covering of gems and gold, Israel also began to focus on her outward beauty instead of cherishing the inner beauty that comes only from a close, dependent relationship with Christ (Eze. 28:13, 17; 16:15). Losing focus of our total need for Christ is always the beginning point of apostasy and idolatry. As Israel forsook the Lord in her heart, notice what she did with the external adornment that God had provided her. *"Thou hast also taken thy fair jewels of my gold and of my silver, which I had given thee, and madest to thyself images of men, and didst commit whoredom with them, and tookest thy broidered garments, and coveredst them: and thou hast set mine oil and mine incense before them. My meat also which I gave thee, fine flour, and oil, and honey, wherewith I fed thee, thou hast even set it before them for a sweet savour: and thus it was, saith the Lord God"* (Eze. 16:17-19). Ezekiel obviously refers here to the ways the pagans worshiped the deities that we discussed earlier. In fact, it was so bad that Israel even began sacrificing their own children in an attempt to obtain the favor of the false gods (verses 20, 21).

One can imagine how sick it made God's heart to view such spiritual darkness among those whom He had clothed with the glorious light of truth about Himself. But as for the jewelry, we see that in this context it only became defiled when false worship began to creep in.

In fact, we end our study of Ezekiel 16 with the Lord telling Israel that He will use those very pagan nations that Israel sought to imitate to strip them of their clothes, take their "fair jewels," and leave them "naked and bare" (verse 39). In essence, by their unfaithfulness they lost that which God had given them in the beginning of their relationship. "They will throw their silver into the streets, and their gold will be an unclean thing. Their silver and their gold will not be able to save them in the day of the Lord's wrath. . . . For it has made them stumble into sin. *They were proud of their beautiful jewelry and used it to make their detestable idols and vile images.* Therefore [or because of this] I will turn these [the jewels] into an unclean thing for them" (Eze. 7:19, 20, NIV).

## *The Heart of the Issue*

The best biblical instruction for discarding jewelry appears in the New Testament. We will look at two passages, one by Paul and the other by Peter. "I also want women to dress modestly, with decency and propriety, not with braided hair or gold or pearls or expensive clothes, but with good deeds, appropriate for women who profess to worship God" (1 Tim. 2:9, 10, NIV). "Your beauty should not come from outward adornment, such as braided hair and the wearing of gold jewelry and fine clothes. Instead, it should be that of your inner self, the unfading beauty of a gentle and quiet spirit, which is of great worth in God's sight. For this is the way the holy women of the past who put their hope in God used to make themselves beautiful" (1 Peter 3:3-5, NIV).

Here we have presented the real nuts and bolts of the issue. The apostles, from their studies of Old Testament history, have laid out for us a great principle that we can use as a guide in determining how to relate to external adornment. The wise man also stated the same principle when he wrote: "Charm is deceptive, and beauty is fleeting; but a woman who fears the Lord is to be praised" (Prov. 31:30, NIV).

The heart of the issue is really an issue of the heart! In other words, does our heart find its value by being adorned with spiritual attributes, or do we seek through external show to prove that we are somebody valuable? Perhaps the deepest thrust of this principle, as it pertains to jewelry, is that we often use it as a substitute for Christ in an attempt to establish some human self-worth. This too is a species of idolatry. The Lord desires for His children to find their self-worth in the price that He paid for them in the person of His Son, Jesus Christ.

Peter and Paul both point out the fallacy of trusting external adornment (or anything else, for that matter) for a sense of importance and virtue. They remind us that genuine virtue is always found on the inside and not on the outside. Though antijewelry advocates often use these texts as absolute decrees against physical adornment, they really state that as people become more and more infatuated with Jesus Christ on the inside, they become less and less concerned about having to prove anything outwardly. In other words, they die to self. It is the natural outworking of an inner principle.

The apostles are simply addressing the same question Jeremiah raised when he asked, "What are you doing, O devasted one? Why dress yourself in scarlet and put on jewels of gold? Why shade your eyes with paint? You adorn yourself in vain" (Jer. 4:30, NIV). Scripture is crystal clear on this point. It is nothing more than fading vanity to deck ourselves out with ornaments just so we can feel a little more secure about ourselves. It is putting trust not in God but in perishable material and is comparable to the Israelites fashioning their jewels into images of their false gods.

There never has been and never will be any protection in self-adornment. We are safe only as we allow God to adorn us. Just as He in the beginning ornamented Lucifer with gold and precious stones (Eze. 28) and as He symbolically decorated Israel with all manner of precious material (Eze. 16), so the Lord seeks to cover us with the ornaments of a converted heart, the fruits of the Spirit of God (Gal. 5:22, 23). While the world strives to obtain a perishable crown, the Christian's focus is on the crown of eternal life that will never perish. "Now they do it to obtain a corruptible crown, but we an uncorruptible" (1 Cor. 9:25).

Especially today, in light of the ever-growing piercing craze going on in our society and the constant emergence of gaudy public figures, I ask, Would our Christian witness of total dependence on Christ be stronger by wearing fewer of the things the world trusts in? May God grant Christians today the courage to stand up and be "a holy nation, His own special people, that you may proclaim the praises of Him who called you out of darkness into His marvelous light" (1 Peter 2:9, NKJV). We don't need the piercing of our ears, lips, nose, and navel as much as we need the piercing of our heart with godly repentance. As it is written: "Rend your heart and not your garments" (Joel 2:13).

But I also want us to see that the pride factor, as it relates to jewelry, can be a two-edged sword. Not long ago I attended a group study during which someone stated that if people wore jewelry it automatically indicated that they were either proud or promiscuous. I strongly objected to such blanket judgments. When are we ever going to learn the first lesson we should have acquired way back in Christianity 101—"Judge not, that ye be not judged" (Matt. 7:1)? Such sweeping declarations indicate that we have just pushed Christ off His judgment throne and are attempting to rule the universe ourselves.

The truth of the matter is that just as much pride—if not more—can reign in someone's heart over the fact that they *don't* wear jewelry. Especially in ultraconservative Adventist circles, in which some seem more interested in checking how well they are doing in the standards game than they are in laboring for those outside their compound, it is easy to feel secure in conformity to peer pressure. Actually, in this case the real humility test might be to attend one of such gatherings dressed in a manner that does not fit in with the crowd.

Spiritual pride can sometimes hide itself in the most inconspicuous ways. Just as some cover up their lack of relationship with Christ (pride) with outward adornment, conservative Christians can cover up their void of Christ (pride) by abstaining from ornaments. If not handed over to God at conversion, mortal pride will simply transfer itself from external adornment to other areas such as pride in our spiritual knowledge or our outward show of compliance to standards.

Though we may fool even our own selves with such fig leaf garments, God knows what we are really like. And He desperately tries to help us see our condition. That's why we need the Word of God. It has the ability to cut through even our religious externals and "judges the thoughts and attitudes of our heart. Nothing in all creation is hidden from God's sight. Everything is uncovered and laid bare before the eyes of Him to whom we must give account"

(Heb. 4:12, 13, NIV). In the final judgment by the One who cannot err, I believe that we will discover that some of the very ones in our church who make such a noise regarding the jewelry question are eaten up with the cancer of their own forms of spiritual pride.

As for the promiscuity charge, coming from the Baptist Church I know multitudes of elderly women who wear jewelry, and I can promise you that sex is the last thing on their minds! Oh sure, it can be used for that purpose. But it is certainly not our place to judge anyone's motives except our own.

Once again we come back around to the motive of why we do what we do. As we have already discovered from the Bible, jewelry of itself is not bad or sinful. It is the motive behind its use that should be in question. God made this precious material for humanity's practical use and enjoyment. He is not the one who has a problem with jewelry—people do. It is what we make out of it that defiles it.

In a sense our condition is like the diabetic. Because of their illness their body cannot appropriately handle honey and other foods that contain sugar. Though there is nothing inherently bad about honey, for the diabetic it can be extremely detrimental. Likewise, we are all sick with sin. Therefore materialism, whether it be in the form of jewels, money, lavish homes, fancy cars, or anything else that surrounds us in our materialistic age, can be spiritually harmful to us because of our tendency to indulge those things sinfully. Materialism among God's people in Ezekiel's day made them stumble into sin (Eze. 7:19, 20). So while we are ill with sin, the best policy for most of us is to be extremely cautious how we relate to jewels and precious stones and as much as possible minimize their use. But after Jesus comes and He has cured our sinful natures, then God's Word says that He will entrust us with these good things because we will then be able to handle them properly.

What's more, certain people seem to have an immunity to the effects of some things that would cause the downfall of someone else. For example, unlimited financial resources could lead many people away from God, but Abraham and Job remained steadfast despite it. Is it too far-fetched, then, to think that there may be someone whose commitment to God would remain unaffected if they wore jewelry? What about that big gold chain that the king of Egypt put around Joseph's neck (Gen. 41:42)? Did it affect his commitment to God? If not, then why do we seem to be so intent on telling every Adventist cowboy that it's sinful for him to wear a big buckle? The bottom line is really this: In areas such as the wearing of ornaments it is between the individual and God to determine what they can or cannot handle.

Some of us fear such reasoning. As with the church of the Dark Ages, we are afraid that if our church ever opens the lid on full liberty of conscience we won't be able to get it back on. Though we talk a lot about religious liberty, we Adventists really fear the ramifications of what we preach. We shrink back in horror at the thought of where it might lead. So we try to strain the meaning of certain scriptures to support our traditional conclusions on such subjects as jewelry. We even go so far as to manipulate people's consciences by refusing them baptism if they don't discard all jewelry, even though not a single place in the Bible or the writings of Ellen White tells us we should follow such a course. Though we often pride ourselves that we are a people of the Word, when faced with such challenges we too will reach for our *Church Manual* to establish our rules for faith. The reality is that we actually water down the real convicting principles of God's Word by trying to use our manipulative tactics. Would we not have better success at just presenting the biblical principle and letting the Holy Spirit use His divine sword to cut away at the heart?

One very well-known conservative leader in our church told me recently, "Keavin, I'm afraid we've lost the battle over jewelry in the Adventist Church." He confided that he had reached his conclusion after realizing the lack of real scriptural evidence to support a hard-line position on the subject. Which might be a good time for me to make a personal confession.

I'm sure that some who don't know me are by now thinking I'm some out-of-control liberal. For what it's worth, neither my wife nor I have worn one article of jewelry, other than useful articles such as watches and hair clips, for more than 16 years. We don't even wear wedding bands, even though it would now be perfectly acceptable in our church if we did. To be really honest, I wish we all could just forget the whole issue and be content in looking forward to our heavenly jewels. But I realize that everyone is not like me, and to be even more honest, I'm glad they are not. One thing I have especially come to appreciate about God's arrangement with His creatures is His willingness to allow everyone to think and choose for themselves.

## A Closer Look

Now, I know that someone will insist that the statements we read from 1 Timothy 2 and 1 Peter 3 are ironclad statements that we under no circumstances should wear any physical adornment. Though such a conclusion fits in so well with our traditional views, a more thorough investigation of the passages will reveal that we have been somewhat inconsistent even in our interpretation of them.

Let's start with 1 Peter 3:3, 4. The real intent of the passage is not to condemn externals but rather the subjection of women. Once again, this scriptural instruction could be as easily violated by those who wear no outward adornments as it could by those who do.

We must also take into consideration Peter's admonition that Christian women should make holy women of old, who radiated with inner beauty, their examples rather than the fashion models of the magazine racks. Yet notice the individual whom he suggests as that role model for submission: Sarah, the wife of Abraham (verse 6). Now, remember, this very same Abraham provided jewels for his future daughter-in-law, Rebekah (Gen. 24:22, 30, 53). It may be a matter of speculation, but if Abraham was comfortable in giving jewels, silver, and gold to the one who would become his son's wife, then it is not far-fetched to believe that his own wife probably wore them. On the other hand, if Abraham and Sarah didn't employ adornment, then Abraham must have sent the gifts with his trusted servant in order to meet Rebekah and her family where they were with their customary expectations. If that was the case, then Abraham treated the subject of adornment as one of custom rather than a moral issue. If we still persist with the argument that Sarah and Abraham were products of their time and didn't have the light on adornment, just as they didn't have the light on polygamy, then Peter made a poor choice of a role model to deliver his antiadornment message.

Some argue that in Abraham's day jewelry was their form of currency. "Therefore," they say, "for Abraham's servant to offer jewelry would be comparable to our giving money today." Without doubt, at that time jewelry had monetary value. But Scripture reveals that they also traded in silver and gold as currency besides what was turned into jewels (Gen. 23:16).

Next we have 1 Timothy 2:9, 10. Now, this verse really seems to have some meaning to it regarding the principle of outward adornment. However, once again jewelry is not the focus of Paul's instruction, but rather that women should be silent. It once again amazes me how we treat such passages of Scripture so inconsistently. We strongly emphasize the counsel regarding a woman's outward appearance and tend to condemn those who disregard it, but totally ignore verse 8, which instructs men to lift up their hands while praying. If someone attempted to emphasize this practice in our church, no doubt many would accuse him of trying to bring Pentecostalism into our ranks. And furthermore, if we try to follow the verses literally, why do we have no problem permitting women to teach or even speak in church when it clearly tells us that they should remain silent (verses 11, 12). Of course, it is because most of us understand that this counsel was a product of Timothy's time and was totally appropriate in a society that allowed woman very few privileges.

My point regarding the two passages of scripture is this: Yes, I do believe we find in them a vital principle of simplicity that we need to share with people, but once again I find no reason to use the passages as absolute evidence that God arbitrarily condemns all physical adornment. While we tend to make a forceful rule out of it when dealing with people, the Holy Spirit seeks to work into their hearts the principle of modesty and simplicity that will be like leaven in a lump of dough. What eventually, in time, results are the beautiful, simple attributes of Christ's life formed within the inner person. The focus is then no longer on the exterior, but on what the Lord is doing on the heart. Of course, we will notice a change on the outside, but that transformation will be a genuine one because the Lord brought it about rather than it being the result of human scriptural arm-twisting. Other people will discard any unnecessary adornment because they feel that they don't need it anymore, not because they have to give it up so as to be accepted.

Though we have been greatly inconsistent in our interpretation of the two texts, they still remain as the two great classics to use in teaching others how to relate to the subject of adornment.

## Ellen White on Adornment

Anyone who reads what Ellen White has written on the subject of jewelry and adornment will have no question that she took a very conservative stand against it. It is actually from her, and not Scripture, that the church has historically found its best defense for its strong position on the subject. This is why when those who oppose jewelry realize that many of the biblical arguments we use are weak, they immediately appeal to "Sister White says." But sooner or later every Seventh-day Adventist must ask themselves: "Do we use Ellen White to interpret the meaning of Scripture, or do we use the Scriptures to interpret Ellen White?" That question was an easy one to answer even for Ellen White herself. She said: "The testimonies of Sister White should not be carried to the front. God's Word is the unerring standard. The Testimonies are not to take the place of the Word. . . . *Let all prove their positions from the Scriptures and substantiate every point they claim as truth from the revealed Word of God* " (Ev 256; italics supplied). Again: *"Our position and faith is in the Bible.* And never do we want any soul to bring in the Testimonies ahead of the Bible" (*ibid.;* italics supplied). What is she saying here? She is counseling us never to try to make any more of a case than we can substantiate from the Bible.

Ellen White made her strong statements regarding physical adornment on the basis of the principle of needless adornment discussed in 1 Peter and 1 Timothy. That's the portion of Scripture you will find her appealing to the most. Was she correct in her interpretation of the principle? Absolutely! And it is upon this point and this point alone that we can justifiably use Ellen White's antiadornment counsel. Once again, her work was to call attention to the general principles of the Word of God, not to establish some new hard-line position. Only heaven knows how many honest seekers of truth we have turned away because of what sometimes appears to be our legalistic approach toward their wearing of jewelry.

As seen in her own life and how she treated cases requiring special counsel, even Ellen White's position was not quite as hard-line as some would seek to make it. Take, for example, the issue of the wedding band. Not that long ago the subject became the focus of hot debate in the Adventist Church. Many members of the church felt that the counsel Ellen White gave regarding the use of the wedding band, as recorded in *Testimonies to Ministers* (pp. 180, 181), absolutely condemned it. While she clearly enunciated the principles behind her recommendation that at that time Adventists not wear wedding rings in America, she did state that "in countries where the custom is imperative, we have no burden to condemn those who have their wedding ring; *let them wear it if they can do so conscientiously.*" Her statement reveals that she recognized the ring as an issue of custom and not morality. If the wedding ring were immoral it would have to be so worldwide, but it has been acceptable by our church for years in other countries. When something is not a matter of morality, then it must simply be one of custom.

It was on this basis that the North American Division at their year-end meeting in 1986 made the decision to allow the use of the wedding ring in North America because large numbers of church members from countries where the ring was customary had moved into North America.

Ellen White sometimes wore a rather large brooch. Earlier, in chapter 3, we discussed the case of her gold watch. She said, "some were in trial because Sister White wore gold" (HS 123). No doubt many today who desire absolutes would condemn Ellen White herself if she were still around.

Obviously Ellen White carried out the biblical counsel of not putting on gold for the superficial purpose of beautifying her person because she regarded it as violating a Christian principle. But it cannot be dismissed that she personally had no problem with the wearing of it if it served a useful purpose. Her counsel called for simplicity of dress without "needless adornment" (see OHC 273). She told us the only reason she discarded her gold watch was that other people had a problem with her wearing it, not because she did (HS 123).

Maybe some in our church today who are so adamant that they be allowed to wear things that cause others to stumble could learn a lesson from a true servant of Christ here regarding the unselfish principle of submission. They may triumphantly point to the Bible and say that it does not necessarily condemn the wearing of all jewelry. Undoubtedly they will even use some of the arguments I've made in this chapter as license to decorate their mortal bodies. But to such let me say, If how you use adornment doesn't condemn you in the judgment, a selfish attitude that would cause church members to stumble over it will. Jesus said: "But whoso shall offend one of these little ones which believe in me, it were better for him that a millstone were hanged about his neck, and that he were drowned in the depth of the sea" (Matt. 18:6).

It seems reasonable that we should consider Ellen White's statements regarding the use of bodily ornaments on two fronts. One involves those who have become convicted that Ellen White was a true messenger of light sent from God. If that is the case, then we would do well to heed what God presented through her, taking into consideration the time, place, and circumstances of each particular statement.

The other front concerns those individuals who have not yet come to accept the divine calling of Ellen White's mission. We cannot use her writings with them. "I have been shown that some . . . make the visions a rule by which to measure all, and have taken a course which my husband and myself have never pursued. . . . Those who were, comparatively, strangers to the visions have been dealt with in the same manner as those who have had much light and experience in the visions" (1T 382). God intends that we deal with this class by simply presenting them with the clear principles found in the Bible. We may rest assured that the Holy Spirit will take over from there.

While we should carefully instruct new converts on the subject of idolatrous dress and prepare them for membership in a church that commonly holds that "to dress plainly, and abstain from display of jewelry and ornaments of every kind is in keeping with our faith" (Ev 269), "it is too late now to become enthusiastic in making a test of this matter" (*ibid.* 273). To make such subjects as dress and physical adornment a central issue is not in harmony with the work of the Holy Spirit for this hour. "There are many who try to correct the life of others by attacking what they consider are wrong habits. They go to those whom they think are in error, and point out their defects. They say, 'You don't dress as you should.' *They try to pick off the ornaments,* or whatever seems offensive, but they do not seek to fasten the mind to the truth. *Those who seek to correct others should present the attractions of Jesus.* They should talk of His love and compassion, present His example and sacrifice, reveal His Spirit, and *they need not touch the subject of dress at all.* There is no need to make the dress question the main point of your religion. There is something richer to speak of. Talk of Christ, and *when the heart is converted, everything that is out of harmony with the word of God will drop off.* . . . In order to teach men and women the worthlessness of earthly things, you must lead them to the living Fountain, and get them to drink of Christ, until their hearts are filled with the love of God, and Christ is in them, a well of water springing up into everlasting life" (ST July 1, 1889; italics supplied).

## Conclusion

I realize that what I have just said will challenge many. Believe me when I say that writing on this subject has been one of the most difficult things I have ever attempted. I let a friend of mine read the first draft. The question she asked me was challenging in itself. "What are you trying to prove by writing this?" she asked. I pondered that question for a long time and have decided to present my answer as a conclusion to this chapter.

First, I urge Adventists to be a people who interpret the Bible with integrity. Nothing will ruin our influence with people more quickly than for them to see us as those who wrestle with the contextual meaning of a Bible verse for the purpose of supporting one of our peculiar positions. Also, calmly laying out the biblical principles on a subject and allowing the Lord to work that principle into the life of the person with whom we are laboring has a sacred power in itself. We often interrupt the sacred communion between the Lord and our evangelistic interests by trying to manipulate them through fear, force, or other means of coercion. Instead, we should want the Spirit, not human beings, to generate and inspire conviction. Personal expressions and experiences are fine if we make it plain to the individual that we in no way expect the same of them. We should always encourage them to study the topic for themselves and make their own personal convictions the reason they change instead of just following our example. By writing this chapter I'm in no way suggesting that our emphasis on modesty in adornment is wrong. What I'm attempting to do is to challenge us to find a better way to present it based on sound biblical logic.

Second, I desire that we see people as being more important than our personal beliefs or convictions. Paul made it clear that we can have all knowledge and understand all mysteries, but if we don't possess a genuine interest in other people's rights, then in God's sight we are the ones who have the biggest problem (see 1 Cor. 13). Most people can quickly tell whether we are really interested in them or just in making them an evangelistic trophy. In light of this subject, we should be able to love and respect the one who is all decked out with jewels as much as, if not more than, the one who fits into our Adventist way of thinking. Just because the Adventist Church may lose its battle over jewelry doesn't mean we have to lose the battle over souls.

And last, I have sought in this chapter to help us all realize that a love for Christ should be the real reason for any of us to do what we do. The real issue is not the jewelry—it is Jesus Christ. The devil is always seeking to place our focus on externals. But when we place the love and mercy of Jesus before those who seek something better in life, a supernatural element enters the experience. It produces results that no one can deny. If a person makes changes because Jesus has touched the heart, he or she will stick with their changes even when accused by family or friends of following human or sectarian teachings.

It is painful to realize that some may misunderstand why I have presented what I have. They may think that I have an ulterior motive. But if this particular chapter helps just one person be better able to focus on Jesus in the midst of all the bickering that goes on in the Adventist Church over issues such as jewelry, then the price of being misunderstood has been worth it.

*Chapter Seven*
# Principles of Music

Tension filled the air one Sabbath morning at a local Adventist church I happened to be attending in the Pacific Northwest. The congregation had patiently endured the usual round of preliminaries so common in our worship services. Now the time had arrived for special music. A young woman took her place on the platform and reverently waited for the music sound track to begin. The song started out very softly, but as it progressed it developed a syncopated beat.

In some churches the music would have received its amens, and the service would have continued without any disturbance. But this particular congregation had some members who walked out of the sanctuary in protest. The head elder noticed their obvious dissatisfaction and slipped out the side door to meet them. Then an intense discussion ensued in the foyer of the church.

During the discussion one of the men explained to the elder that the beat of the music reminded him of songs he had listened to in bars before he became a Christian. He had fled such an environment, seeking the church as a refuge from the devil's influence. Now he and his family were fleeing the church because through the music the devil had also established a presence there.

The head elder couldn't identify with the man's reasoning. Having been raised an Adventist, he had never seen the inside of a bar. He had heard music with a beat like that before. But the song that day recalled to his mind the special times he had gathered with friends during vespers while attending a Christian college. He tried sharing his perspective with the offended church member, but to no avail. Though the elder could give a hearty amen to the special music by reason of his own personal experience, the other member could not. Arriving at no other conclusion than that the devil was using that music, the man, along with his family, left.

## A Devisive Issue

Such incidents are not isolated ones. More and more Adventists hotly debate the subject of music. Not only church members, but some leaders as well, have differing opinions as to what constitutes sanctified music. As anyone who has had charge of organizing the music for church convocations will tell you, it is territory filled with explosive land mines of strong opinions. To select music that will satisfy the needs of hundreds, or sometimes even thousands, of people with varying tastes and backgrounds is in itself becoming an art form.

How does one go about deciding what is appropriate or inappropriate Christian music? It is not an easy question to answer. However, in this chapter we will attempt to tackle the issue. Though what I share is obviously not a final word on the subject, it is an honest attempt to seek solutions by trying to help us become more understanding of differing perspectives. After all, if we can't respect the personal convictions of others and are always thinking that we are right and that others need to accept our position, then we automatically hinder God's attempts to unify His remnant people.

To begin with, music is one of the most powerful means of communication. I think everyone will agree to that. The antiestablishment sentiments of 1960s songwriters such as Bob Dylan and John Lennon helped lead a whole generation of young people to protest against the parental and governmental authority of that day. Ellen White has warned us that near the end of time Satan will once again try to use music in deceiving our people to forsake the worship of the true God. Knowing that it is one of the most effective means that we can use to lead the mind to God, he seeks to employ it for his own purposes. "Music was made to serve a holy purpose, to lift the thoughts to that which is pure, noble, and elevating, and to awaken in the soul devotion and gratitude to God. . . . That which is a great blessing when rightly used [music] becomes [by the misuse of it] one of the most successful agencies by which Satan allures the mind from duty and from the contemplation of eternal things" (PP 594).

So let's establish it—and establish it well. The devil does use music to further his satanic warfare. Some forms of music are spiritually deadly. Anyone who denies this fact will sooner or later be led away from God and eternal things.

On the other hand, God also uses music. As a matter of fact, "singing, as a part of religious service, is as much an act of worship as is prayer" *(ibid.)*. The influence of music has led Christians of all ages to a greater commitment to God. Music played a major role in the Protestant Reformation. Leaders such as Martin Luther and Charles Wesley used music to help fan the devotion smoldering in the human heart into a full blaze of dedication to God's holy cause. God can do, and is doing, the same today through people to whom He has given musical talents.

So once again, how do we determine what is appropriate music for Christians to listen to? Actually, the heart of this question identifies the real core of the answer. *In general, we don't determine which music is appropriate or not appropriate for others.* God has set it up through the liberty of individual conscience that ultimately all must decide for themselves what is the right music for them. That's because different music affects different minds in different ways. Music that leads you to think godly thoughts may prompt devilish ones in me. If I judge you according to my experience, then am I not playing the role of God in your life?

It is a serious issue, because like most other lifestyle standards it falls into the arena of religious liberty. Before God, each individual has certain "unalienable rights," one of which is to worship God according to the dictates of his or her own conscience, not according to the conscience of someone else. And since music is a form of worship, my right to listen to whatever I desire is guaranteed me not only by my nation's government, but by the government of heaven as well.

Numerous musical gurus in the Adventist Church will disagree with me on this point. Usually found among the more conservative class, they see it as dangerous to advocate religious liberty in the area of music. To their way of thinking, the suggestion that people should determine for themselves what is good or bad music borders on infidelity. They are more comfortable if they can publicly dictate to our people their understanding of what is safe to listen to and what is not. But I'm telling you, this is nothing short of spiritual dictatorship! If we can control the people's minds through the manipulation of their consciences, then we can better regulate their religious experience.

I will admit that to suggest that we need to let the people decide what music is best for them is a frightening thing, but it's God's way. We must never seek to come between anyone and God with our personal opinions and convictions. Yes, we need to share with others what we believe to be the principles of the matter, but the decision must remain between the individual and God. The bottom line is that they all will reap the harvest of their own choices. The decision each person makes in regard to the music they listen to will ultimately have its impact, either leading them closer to God or farther away from Him.

"Well," someone says, "I'm at least going to choose for my children the kind of music they listen to." Yes, you can and should while they are young and in their formative years. That is the best time to train their musical taste buds. But as parents of every generation will testify, you can do this only up to a certain age. After that, the children will determine for themselves their own personal standard in such matters. Now I again ask: If God hasn't even given us absolute control over our own children's listening habits, what makes us think He is leading us to make a blanket statement on music standards for a church filled with adults? Yet some feel God is calling them to exactly that duty. No doubt such misguided zeal, while it seeks to cleanse the church as Jehu tried to do with Israel, will actually increase division among church members.

Some people see things only in black and white. They desire absolutes and struggle with the thought of gray areas. Not long ago a couple approached me with concerns over some drama presentations that had taken place in their church. They felt that Ellen White had made it clear that any dramatization was of the devil. I tried to explain, as it is with music, that it's the nature of the impressions the drama makes that determines whether it is good or bad.

At this point the man said to me, "If I follow your reasoning, everyone would be a law unto themselves, because there would be no blacks or whites. I guess then our church members can go out and start committing adultery, and there would be no moral boundaries to guide them except their own opinions."

"Come on now," I responded. "Think about it for a moment. Of course God's laws have some black-and-white guidelines. But not everything is that way. For example, I don't think there can be such a thing as Christian pornography, because all pornography leads to evil results. But there can be sanctified Christian drama, because not all drama leaves evil impressions."

The truth of the whole matter is that many individuals have appointed themselves as "definers of the law." They usually have an accompanying spirit that has little tolerance for the rightful convictions of the consciences of others.

## The Most Powerful Principle

I have discussed this issue with multitudes of people who hold varying opinions and tastes in their music appreciation. Some strictly prefer traditional hymns. Others like classical or Renaissance selections. Still others are becoming more and more open to today's myriad styles of contemporary Christian music. I have for a long time been taking inventory of the reasons people give for the music they enjoy listening to. As a result, I have come to the profound conclusion that the most powerful principle that determines which music is healthy for the soul is the principle of association. What a particular song or arrangement triggers in an individual's mind determines whether that music is good or bad for that person. This is why the same song took one man's mind back to his barroom days, while it reminded another man of his cherished experience at a Christian college.

Take, for example, the song called "Morning Has Broken." It appears in the present Seventh-day Adventist hymnal. But some will always remember it as a 1970s hit by pop singer Cat Stevens. Now, let's say that a church member in their late 40s hears that song. It may take their minds back to a time when they were engaged in a lifestyle of free sex and pot parties. Those scenes are ones they would rather forget, but the song triggers them.

Then their teenage son brings home a new Michael Card CD with a release of "Morning Has Broken." The father considers it the devil's music because of what he associates it with. The son, however, doesn't get the same message from the song, because he has never even had sex or attended a pot party. To him the music lifts his thoughts up to Jesus. Nevertheless, the father is adamant that he will allow no satanic music in his house!

Now, I want to ask a question. Who wins in such a scenario? If you answered, "the devil," I believe you are right. While the father feels satisfied that he has stood solid for a holy standard, Satan knows he has succeeded in placing another wedge between the father and his boy. But a sadder thing is yet to come. Some day, when the father will need to use his relationship in order to steer his son aright regarding more important decisions of life, he will discover to his sorrow that his influence in the boy's life has eroded away.

Being a parent myself, I too have a concern for music and any of its promoters who advocate bizarre behavior. Every day we hear songs on our nation's airwaves advocating murder, suicide, divorce, violence, and a host of other immoral behavior. Some contemporary artists in the Christian music world, by their example, advocate body jewelry, tattoos, unusual hairstyles, and other lifestyle patterns that appear to border even on the occult. When the instruments and loud screaming eclipse the intended message, then it matters not to me if the song is supposed to be about Jesus. I personally have a problem with it.

Once again, I'm not advocating a position in which anything and everything goes. What I am trying to do is caution against a witch hunt mentality that would lead us automatically to condemn anything that may savor of something we ourselves are not familiar or comfortable with. We must get over this superstition that if the music makes the toe tap it has to be of the devil. Does the devil work through music? Absolutely! But when we try to read the devil into everything that we are not culturally used to, we are sure to go to extremes.

We must never forget that God is the Alpha and the Omega. He experienced the beginning, "when the morning stars sang together," and He's already visited the end. Therefore, God is not limited to a certain style of a certain age in the past. New and fresh every morning, He has the ability to adapt Himself to the needs of each and every new generation, thus meeting them where they are. While He uses the spiritual classics of the past, He also employs music contemporary to our age to reach today's young people with the message of His love and saving power. Let us, who are their spiritual guardians, be praying for discernment so that we will not stand in God's way.

The rule of thumb I suggest for discerning an acceptable standard for each individual is once again the principle of association. A safe and guiding light in applying that principle is found in *The Acts of the Apostles*. Commenting on the apostle Peter's teaching when he said "Gird up the loins of your mind," Ellen White wrote: "The apostle sought to teach the believers how important it is to keep the mind from wandering to forbidden themes or spending its energies on trifling subjects. Those who would not fall a prey to Satan's devices must guard well the avenues of the soul; *they must avoid reading, seeing, or hearing that which will suggest impure thoughts.* The mind must not be left to dwell at random upon every subject that the enemy of souls may suggest" (p. 518; italics supplied). It is wise counsel from our loving God, who wants no harm to come to any of us.

Do you see the corridor of individuality in the counsel? Though many conclude it to be a black-and-white statement, that is not necessarily the case. Like most other statements, different people will apply it in different ways, according to the principle of association. Now, if we are again talking about the use of pornographic pictures, then I would say yes, it will only tend to corrupt all who look. In this case, a blanket standard would be applicable. But I do not believe one can apply the same rationale to music, even though many do. Here once again a certain song or style that suggests impure thoughts to my mind may lift your thoughts up to Jesus.

## *Music for Worship*

Now, back to that disagreement between the head elder and the church member who became offended over the music that day in the Pacific Northwest. What can we possibly do in churches in which the debate over music threatens the harmony of the worship service? Though I don't want to be so naïve as to think there is some magical solution to this difficulty, I would like to make some observations and suggestions.

To begin with, the purpose of a divine worship service is to worship God. True worship can happen only as a congregation is unified in both spirit and truth. Anything that interrupts this unity will destroy the heavenly atmosphere of worship. Thus it is vital that as worshipers we bring to the sanctuary not only a reverent attitude toward God, but a Christlike spirit toward those with whom we worship. Once again it means that we be sensitive to those things that might offend others—in this case, music.

For churches struggling with the problem of music sensitivity, perhaps the church board could design a plan that attempts to satisfy the peculiarities of the local congregation. Churches, like individuals, have different characteristics. What may prove to be appropriate in one church may be totally out of place in another. For example, a church in Alabama may find a country, folk style as simply being in harmony with Southern gospel tradition, whereas a church in the Boston area might view such sounds as unsanctified. Each board must determine the particular musical definitions of its church.

However, I must sound a caution here. Individual board members must not base their vote solely on their personal opinions of what is proper or improper music. If the plan is to succeed at all, it must be approached objectively, taking into consideration the overall needs of the congregation at large. We can accomplish this only by allowing all church members who desire so to express their views on the subject.

I may be a board member who enjoys listening to a certain style of music in my home or car. But if I think the music would cause controversy at my church, then I should make the mature decision that it is inappropriate and vote accordingly.

If I perform the music for the worship service and find out that a drumbeat off a sound track offends some, then maybe I should choose something from the *Seventh-day Adventist Hymnal*. (By the way, we can be thankful for our current hymnal, which offers a wide variety of songs that all can be blessed by.)

Or perhaps I discomfort some by the way I use certain gestures to express my personal emotion about a song. In that case maybe the thing to do would be to seek to bring less notice to myself and how I feel about the piece. I know this is difficult for some singers, but after all, isn't the purpose of special musical numbers to draw people's attention to Jesus, and not to the human instrument? On the other hand, those who don't get easily worked up over a song need to empathize with those whose emotions are more apt to take control.

Now, as I said, all of these things are mere suggestions. I'm aware that it is the ideal and that it is highly unlikely that any plan implemented by a church board will please all the members. But it's better than just letting a church splinter. If the church does come up with a plan and it receives strong opposition, then handle it with kid gloves. Carefully explain to the opposing elements the purpose behind the board's democratic decision. If they refuse to accept the plan, then they willfully choose to become a disorganizing element to the body. The power lies in the voice of the church proper and should maintain rule over a few disgruntled members.

## A Personal Experience

B efore concluding, I would like to share a personal story regarding the power of musical association.

I grew up in a rural farming community in western Kentucky. It laid my foundation of simple living and religious thought. My early years I spent freely roaming my family's 400-acre farm and attending the local Baptist church. For the most part it was a life of relative innocence, which unknowingly I would later associate with the old Protestant hymns we sang.

Subsequent years would take me far away from my old Kentucky home, my Baptist heritage, and my childhood innocence. There was a big world waiting, and I set out early to explore it. In the process I also wandered far away from the God of my youth and even began imbibing atheistic concepts. But the Lord had a time, a place, and a song chosen that He knew would one day bring me home to Him.

In 1985, after nearly 10 years of godless living, I ended up in spiritual bankruptcy. It was then that my wife and I met a certain Adventist family. I shared with them some of my struggles, and they invited us to their home in the Tennessee countryside for the weekend. It was in the autumn of the year, about harvesttime.

That Sabbath we spent fasting and praying that the Lord would restore to me the hope of my salvation. As the day wore into the afternoon, we gathered on the living room floor of their old farmhouse, much like the one I grew up in. The time came when I began to pour out my soul to God. It was a real struggle for me. Peeling back the chapters of my life was a painful ordeal. I felt I was too great a sinner for the Lord ever to accept me again.

While I was praying, the family's 9-year-old daughter started, I suppose out of boredom, swinging on the front porch. Before long, with an angelic simplicity that could only come from a child, she began to sing softly, "'All to Jesus I surrender, all to Him I freely give; I will ever love and trust Him, in His presence daily live; I surrender all, I surrender all; all to Thee, my blessed Saviour, I surrender all.'"

As the words of that unstaged song floated through the screened windows it took my mind back to my own childhood days of innocence. I remembered how I had loved the Lord as a little boy and had been baptized at 11. Then I vividly saw how little by little I began to stray until I finally landed in a scary sinful world with no hope of a better one. I realized how I had for years hurt so many people through my sinful influence. But now, for the first time, I came face-to-face with the reality of how I had disappointed that great God who had hung on Calvary for me.

A flood of emotion began to overwhelm me. I left the house and began walking back through an open field. There, alone, in the quiet of nature, I knelt down under a maple tree blazing with the rich colors of autumn and prayed. I remember asking God to forgive my life of sinfulness and restore to me the happiness and innocence of my youth. His reply to my mind was, "Keavin, you're still My little boy. How would you like for your life record up to this point to be gone? If you want, I'll grant you a clean slate and let you grow up all over again."

Suddenly I felt just as Scripture said I would—like a new creature. God had answered my prayer. The weight of my old life lifted. All the stains and shame of my horrid past were no longer counted against me, and now I could live differently. As I opened my eyes, it was amazing how everything about me seemed beautiful and innocent. Opening my Bible, for the first time I read it and clearly understood each word, as though it had been written just for me. "Therefore, since Christ suffered for us in the flesh, arm yourselves also with the same mind, for he who has suffered in the flesh has ceased from sin, that he no longer should live the rest of his time in the flesh for the lusts of men, but for the will of God. For we have spent enough of our past lifetime in doing the will of the Gentiles— when we walked in lewdness, lusts, drunkenness, revelries, drinking parties, and abominable idolatries. In regard to these, they think it strange that you do not run with them in the same flood of dissipation, speaking evil of you. . . . But the end of all things is at hand; therefore be serious and watchful in your prayers" (1 Peter 4:1-7, NKJV). Though I knew that I would most likely lose every friend I had made up to that point in my life, it didn't matter as long as I knew I had a new life with Christ.

The events of that Sabbath day 16 years ago changed the course of my life. As long as I live, I will always remember it as the major turning point in my life. It was the day God spoke to me through a song.

*Chapter Eight*
# Principles of Health

The history of Seventh-day Adventism has certainly had its share of extreme mind-sets in the area of lifestyle standards. If we were honest, we would all admit that we have been prone to it at some point in our experience. Those who grew up outside the church often go overboard when they first begin reading Ellen White's counsels, while those reared under the influence of "Sister White says" often swing toward the liberal end of the spectrum once they get old enough to decide for themselves. Certainly "there is in human nature a tendency to run to extremes and from one extreme to another entirely opposite" (5T 305).

Yet I am encouraged as I watch the tension of conflicting viewpoints struggling both in individuals and in the church at large. Experiencing such extremes is often the necessary process some need go through in order to find a balance. As a result, I believe we will one day see emerge from Adventism some of the most spiritually balanced, biblically based people who have ever been part of God's cause on earth. Like the monarch butterfly, whose wings develop for flight only through an intense struggle to free itself from its cocoon, so do God's people gain spiritual balance by struggling to escape the extreme positions they've adopted.

Perhaps in no area of lifestyle have we as many extreme beliefs as in the area of health. While some try to treat it as irrelevant to their spirituality, others relate to it as though it is the determining factor in their salvation. Ellen White's health counsels can appear somewhat extreme if one doesn't realize that she wrote certain statements in an attempt to move people to a middle position. She counsels us to "agitate, agitate, agitate" some subjects while at the same time warning us of the dangers of taking her counsel too far. No doubt both camps would be wise to follow her counsel not to "go into the water, or into the fire, but take the middle path, avoiding all extremes" (CD 211).

Though the church at large has managed to stay steady and remain on the cutting edge of health research and education through its fine medical institutions, it continuously suffers disrepute because of the unwise actions of individual church members who become overzealous about her health counsels. Ellen White has warned that such behavior will discredit the church in the area of health. "There will be some who will not leave the best and most correct impression upon minds. *They will be inclined to narrow ideas and plans,* and have not the least idea of what constitutes health reform. *They will take the testimonies which have been given for special individuals under particular circumstances, and make these testimonies general and to apply in all cases,* and in this way they bring discredit upon my work and the influence of the testimonies upon health reform" (3SM 288; italics supplied). On the other hand, those members who disregard the health message altogether also embarrass the church.

A close connection exists between extreme teachings in health and extreme positions in theology. In my travels I have mentally cataloged some of the sentiments I've heard expressed that illustrate this point. Once in answer to the question "How are we saved?" a Sabbath school participant answered that if we don't gain control over our appetites, we will be lost. I've heard it said that "people who eat meat aren't really Adventists." An Adventist pastor once told his congregation that the message of health reform was the third angel's message "in verity." Another man I met several years ago advocated fruitarianism because he interpreted Ellen White's statements about God's plan to lead humanity back to the original diet given in Eden to mean the exclusion of even vegetables from our tables (see CD 380; taken in context, the Edenic diet was just another one of Mrs. White's ways to advocate a menu free from meat). Hang around long enough, and you can expect anything when it comes to well-meaning people advocating extreme teachings in health.

# A Gospel Perspective

I would like to begin our discussion on health, specifically dietary habits, by placing it in a gospel perspective. The apostle Paul exhorted us to "accept Christians who are weak in faith, and don't argue with them about what they think is right or wrong. For instance, one person believes it is all right to eat anything. But another believer who has a sensitive conscience will eat only vegetables. Those who think it is all right to eat anything must not look down on those who won't. And those who won't eat certain foods must not condemn those who do, for God has accepted them. Who are you to condemn God's servants? They are responsible to the Lord, so let him tell them whether they are right or wrong. The Lord's power will help them do as they should. . . . Those who eat all kinds of food do so to honor the Lord, since they give thanks to God before eating. And those who won't eat everything also want to please the Lord and give thanks to God. . . . So why do you condemn another Christian? Why do you look down on another Christian? Remember, each of us will stand personally before the judgment seat of God. For the Scriptures say, 'As surely as I live,' says the Lord, 'every knee will bow to me and every tongue will confess allegiance to God.' Yes, each of us will have to give a personal account to God. So don't condemn each other anymore. Decide instead to live in such a way that you will not put an obstacle in another Christian's path. I know and am perfectly sure on the authority of the Lord Jesus that no food, in and of itself, is wrong to eat. But if someone believes it is wrong, then for that person it is wrong. And if another Christian is distressed by what you eat, you are not acting in love if you eat it. Don't let your eating ruin someone for whom Christ died. Then you will not be condemned for doing something you know is all right. For the Kingdom of God is not a matter of what we eat or drink, but of living a life of goodness and peace and joy in the Holy Spirit. If you serve Christ with this attitude, you will please God. And other people will approve of you, too. So then, let us aim for harmony in the church and try to build each other up. Don't tear apart the work of God over what you eat. Remember, there is nothing wrong with these things in themselves. But it is wrong to eat anything if it makes another person stumble. Don't eat meat or drink wine or do anything else if it might cause another Christian to stumble. You may have the faith to believe that there is nothing wrong with what you are doing, but keep it between yourself and God. Blessed are those who do not condemn themselves by doing something they know is all right. But if people have doubts about whether they should eat something, they shouldn't eat it. They would be condemned for not acting in faith before God. If you do anything you believe is not right, you are sinning" (Rom. 14, NLT).

Now, I know that we Adventists are not really comfortable with this passage. However, I chose it because it deals with a greater issue than what we eat or don't eat—individual liberty of conscience. So often those on fire for health reform overlook this issue. If they adopt a health program, then they feel everyone else must follow their example exactly. Yet God doesn't see it that way. His relationship with each person is as though he or she were the only one living on earth (see SC 100).

In addition, some in the church seek to make health a test for others in their acceptance of Christ. However, Ellen White has reminded us that such issues are between the individual and God, and we are not to use them as human-made tests. "Do you not remember that we have an individual accountability? *We do not make articles of diet a test question,* but we do try to educate the intellect, and to arouse the moral sensibility to take hold of health reform in an intelligent manner, as Paul represents it in Romans 13:8-14; 1 Corinthians 9:24-27; 1 Timothy 3:8-12" (CD 466; italics supplied). As we look up these references from the apostle Paul we will discover stated principles, not a list of specifics.

## Health Deform

Different people have different needs and tastes. "There is real common sense in health reform. People cannot all eat the same things. Some articles of food that are wholesome and palatable to one person may be hurtful to another. Some cannot use milk, while others can subsist upon it. For some, dried beans and peas are wholesome, while others cannot digest them. Some stomachs have become so sensitive that they cannot make use of the coarser kind of graham flour. *So it is impossible to make an un-*

*varying rule by which to regulate everyone's dietetic habits"* (CH 154,155; italics supplied).

For example, many take Ellen White's statements about removing dairy products from the diet and think it is the message of the hour. Their burden is to lead others to give up their use, yet they give no adequate warning of the risk of vitamin $B_{12}$ deficiency. I know a prominent Adventist health promoter who convinced a young woman to discard all dairy products from her diet. He also told her that her body would naturally produce enough $B_{12}$ and therefore she didn't need to supplement it. Later the woman began having digestive and elimination problems. The same health promoter then suggested that her difficulties probably resulted from candida and ordered her not to eat any sweets, including fruits. Her condition worsened during the following months until she discovered that the real problem was a $B_{12}$ deficiency. A simple, inexpensive supplement remedied her disorders within a week! (The use of vitamin $B_{12}$ supplements containing cyanocobalamin is an intelligent decision on the part of those who choose to delete all animal products from their diet.)

Such stories unfortunately are not rare. Once a physician named Daniel Kress took Ellen White's counsels regarding the deletion of dairy products to the ultimate extreme. His health broke down to the point where he lay near death. Someone contacted Ellen White by letter in Australia and notified her of the doctor's condition. The following is a portion of the letter she wrote to him: "Do not put yourself through [such an extreme regimen] as you have done, and do not go to extremes in regard to the health reform. Some of our people are very careless in regard to health reform. But because some are far behind, you must not, in order to be an example to them, be an extremist. You must not deprive yourself of that class of food which makes good blood. *Your devotion to true principles is leading you to submit yourself to a diet which is giving you an experience that will not recommend health reform.* This is your danger. When you see that you are becoming weak physically, it is essential for you to make changes, and at once. Put into your diet something you have left out. It is your duty to do this. Get eggs of healthy fowls. Use these eggs cooked or raw. Drop them uncooked into the best unfermented wine you can find. This will supply that which is necessary to your system. *Do not for a moment suppose that it will not be right to do this"* (12MR 168).

Evidently Ellen White realized that he had become so entrenched in an extreme mind-set about how bad dairy products were that she had to say, "do not for a moment suppose that it will not be right to do this." Of course we do not know for sure, but some health experts view the incident as a classic case of vitamin $B_{12}$ deficiency. We do know that Dr. Kress followed her advice and recovered his health. He also continued his prescribed regimen of eggs and grape juice for the rest of his life, dying in 1956 at the ripe old age of 94.

I know of others who advocate dispensing with vegetable oil based on a single statement Ellen White made that we should use "oil, as eaten in the olive" (CD 350). Disregarding evidence that the White Estate possesses receipts from Ellen White's household records showing the purchase of large quantities of cooking oil, they try to prove that she meant that we shouldn't use extracted oils. I also know of individuals who wound up hospitalized for malnourishment and had their doctors order them to incorporate fat into their diet. Such cases can hardly be good advertisements for Adventist health programs. (Note: We should also point out that Ellen White's statements against the use of "grease" refers to animal fats, not vegetable fats.)

What leads many into such extremes is that they treat Ellen White's comments about health as though they were commandments written in stone. Have you ever met someone who considers eating ice cream or a third meal as a violation of the commandment against murder? I have! (I'm not necessarily recommending ice cream, but just trying to make a point.) Oh, and by the way, what is so unhealthful about ice cream is not a scoop or two, but someone sitting down and knocking off a half gallon! It was the effects of "large quantities of milk and sugar" that Ellen White warned against (CD 330). But for those who feel the need to stay away from ice cream altogether, that's OK too. God has provided some wonderful alternatives in our modern culinary world.

Ellen White wrote many of her health counsels for people with particular problems, much like Paul's suggestion to Timothy to take "a little wine" for his stomach ailments (1 Tim. 5:23). One of the first avenues to imbalance is people taking such circumstantial counsels and trying to give them broad application to everyone. An example is when some have employed her statement regarding the mixture of fruit and vegetables at a meal as being unhealthful and making it a mandate for humanity, when in actuality it was helpful counsel given for those who have weak digestion.

Another sign of imbalance occurs when someone adopts health reform and begins to focus on how the rest of the church is not living up to it. Satan magnifies it in the person's mind to the point that he or she causes division in the church. Believe me, this is not what Ellen White meant by "agitate, agitate, agitate." She simply meant for us to go about promoting the issue in a positive, winsome way. In other words, don't let the issue die out in the church, but keep it before the people. When we use health reform as a holy hammer on the anvil of another's mind, we work against God and disgust people more than win them. Then to comfort our fanatical minds we tell ourselves that they just weren't interested in changing their lifestyle. May God once again help us see that people are more important than health reform. If we present such reform in a right way, nearly everyone will sooner or later (perhaps after their third bypass) catch on.

What it all boils down to is that what people eat is a personal issue between them and God. I know this comes as disappointing news to those who love to lead potluck patrols, but we will be happier once we come to grips with the fact. The only time it becomes our duty to get involved in other people's dietary considerations is when doors open for us to play an educating role on the subject, whether that be in public or in private. However, it does not mean that we go bursting through doors uninvited. No true education can possibly take place under such circumstances. It is the threshhold at which health reform ceases to advance.

## The Meat Issue

In the area of health reform we need to educate people with sound biblical reasoning. Making invalid claims as to what the Bible requires discredits the health message.

I recently saw a billboard with a big picture of Jesus. The message read: "Jesus Was a Vegetarian." I was thankful to see that an animal rights activist group and not Adventists had sponsored it. But we also make some pretty illogical biblical arguments in an attempt to prove that God requires vegetarianism of people. We cite such examples as the antediluvian diet and the prophet Daniel's refusal to eat the king's meat. To the thinking mind the question arises, If God requires that these Old Testament examples be strictly followed, why did He Himself not practice them when He lived His life on earth? The Bible teaches that Jesus not only ate fish and roasted lamb, but He also served it to others (Luke 24:42; John 21:12, 13).

Though the Bible shows the benefits of a vegetarian diet (i.e., the decrease of life span after the introduction of flesh foods following the Flood), it does not require it. Our early pioneers realized that even our arguments against the use of unclean meats lacked specific New Testament support. They taught that to use the Levitical dietary restrictions was not a valid argument. Uriah Smith wrote: "We believe there is better ground on which to rest [the prohibition of pork] than the ceremonial law of the former dispensation, for if we take the position that that law is still binding, we must accept it all, and then we shall have more on our hands than we can easily dispose of" ("The Development of Adventist Thinking on Clean and Unclean Meats," White Estate Shelf Document, issued as manuscript release 852).

It may come as a shock to many, as it did to me, to read a letter Ellen White sent in 1882 to her daughter-in-law, Mary Kelsey White. Mary was returning from Oakland to the Whites' Healdsburg home when Ellen White made the following request: "Mary, if you can get me a good box of herrings, fresh ones, please do so. These last ones that Willie [her son] got are bitter and old. If you can buy cans, say, half a dozen cans, of good tomatoes, please do so. We shall need them. *If you can get a few cans of good oysters, get them*" (*ibid.;* italics supplied). Though some would suggest that she was a hypocrite for this, an accurate understanding of her teachings on the subject helps us make sense of her request. "Mrs. White never explicitly declared that the general distinction between clean and unclean meats was one which Seventh-day Adventists were still bound to observe. *Her statements commending the Jewish practice certainly encourage that position, but never made it explicit*" (*ibid.;* italics supplied).

Ellen White, though she advocated discarding the use of flesh food, was not as legalistic about it as some would make it appear.

Although she often wrote about abandoning flesh foods because of increasing disease in animals, not until 1894 did she herself take a stand to eat no more meat. She then realized, perhaps as never before, the need for church leaders such as herself to uphold the highest example of standards before the people. And she stuck with that decision for the remainder of her life.

In his book *Messenger of the Lord,* Herbert Douglass deals once again with the age-old accusation that she was a hypocrite on the meat issue. "This charge is based on the fact that Ellen White was lucid and forthright regarding the danger of meat eating but occasionally ate flesh foods. Her son W.C. [Willie] wrote to G. B. Starr in 1933 that the White family had been vegetarians but not always 'teetotalers' (total abstainers from flesh foods). In 1894, Ellen White wrote to a non-Adventist active in the temperance cause in Australia who had asked about the Adventist position on being 'total abstainers': 'I am happy to assure you that as a denomination we are in the fullest sense total abstainers from the use of spiritous liquors, wine, beer, [fermented] cider, and also tobacco and all other narcotics. . . . *All are vegetarians, many abstaining from the use of flesh food, while others use it in only the most moderate degree.'* Many of Ellen White's strongest statements against meat were written after she had renewed her commitment to total abstinence in 1894. Here we note that *for Ellen White a vegetarian was not necessarily a 'teetotaler,' that is, a total abstainer, but one who did not eat flesh foods as a habit"* (*Messenger of the Lord,* p. 316; italics supplied).

I believe our position of discouraging the consumption of unclean foods is a biblical one. What I am addressing is the ineffective way in which we often try to prove it. Many Christians with whom we study are New Testament-oriented Christians. To expect them to submit because we show them some Old Testament dietary laws is an unrealistic expectation. A more effective approach would be to begin by pointing out New Testament principles regarding God's desire for us to take the best possible care of our physical health. "Know ye not that your body is the temple of the Holy Ghost which is in you, which ye have of God, and ye are not your own? For ye are bought with a price: therefore glorify God in your body" (1 Cor. 6:19, 20). "Whether therefore ye eat, or drink, or whatsoever ye do, do all to the glory of God" (1 Cor. 10:31). After establishing such principles, we can present abundant evidence from modern medical science that more and more declares a vegetarian diet as best for optimum long-term health. Only then can we go to the Old Testament and show how God knew best a long time ago and led His people in the sensible way that science now outlines for us.

Once we show people the logic behind our argument, we can relax and let them choose for themselves and advance at their own pace rather than make dietary restrictions another test for joining the church. As we read earlier: *"We do not make articles of diet a test question, but we try to educate the intellect, and to arouse the moral sensibility* to take hold of health reform in an intelligent manner" (CD 466; italics supplied). This way we don't appear as religious fanatics trying to prove our dietary convictions by the contextual misuse of Scripture, but rather as intelligent people who encourage others to correctly reason from cause to effect. This is educating in right lines.

A true health reformer will always patiently implement the following counsel: "We must go no faster than we can take those with us whose consciences and intellects are convinced of the truths we advocate. *We must meet the people where they are.* Some of us have been many years in arriving at our present position in health reform. It is a slow work to obtain a reform in diet. . . . If we should allow the people as much time as we have required to come up to the present advanced state in reform, *we would be very patient with them, allowing them to advance step-by-step, as we have done,* until their feet are firmly established upon the health reform platform. *But we should be very cautious not to advance too fast.* . . . If we come to persons who have not been enlightened in regard to health reform, and present our strongest positions at first, *there is danger of their becoming discouraged as they see how much they have to give up,* so that they will make no effort to reform. *We must lead the people along patiently and gradually, remembering the hole of the pit when we were digged"* (CD 468, 468; italics supplied).

## Causing Others to Stumble

In one area, though, what an individual chooses to eat does go beyond their relationship with God. Paul reminds us that "it is wrong to eat anything if it makes another person stumble. Don't eat meat or drink wine or do anything else if it might cause another Christian to stumble. You may have the faith to believe that there is nothing wrong with what you are doing, but keep it between yourself and God" (Rom. 14:20-22, NLT).

Now, I know from personal experience that this principle is easier to say than it is to carry out. A few years ago I spoke at a conference camp meeting. In fact, I visited several camp meetings that summer and had been gone from home several weeks. One thing I don't like about such trips is that it means being away from my wife's cooking.

One particular morning at this camp meeting I woke up late and rushed to the cafeteria before my morning meeting. But I was so late that they had already begun clearing the food away, so all I found was an apple and a bowl of granola. As I sat down to eat, some people who had been attending my meetings sat down to talk with me. The discussion took preeminence over my breakfast, and I don't think I even finished my apple before I had to leave to make my morning appointment.

At 11:00 I spoke to the general assembly for worship. Finishing up shortly after 12:00, I was ravenous with hunger. With several hundred other people I filed out across campus to the cafeteria for lunch. As I entered the door my mouth began to water with the smell of my favorite cuisine—Italian food! Nearing the buffet line I could see that the day's special was lasagna.

An elderly woman behind me inquired if I was the young man who had just finished preaching the sermon. I told her I was. She then commented on how much my emphasis on trusting in Christ's merits for salvation had meant to her. About that time we reached the area where we picked up our trays to begin getting our food. I have to admit that my attention was more focused on that lasagna than on our conversation. Then the test came. With only two people between me and that wonderful Italian creation I overheard the little woman say to her husband, "I can't believe they insist on going against Sister White's counsel and put cheese in the lasagna! Haven't they ever read where she said it should never enter the human stomach?"

Now, first of all, let me make it clear that I don't believe Ellen White gave a blanket statement against cheese. The statement the woman had in mind declares: "Cheese should never be introduced into the stomach." "It is wholly unfit for food" (CD 368; a compiler's note on the same page says "This is understood to mean ripened cheese"). She made such warnings against cheese because of its high bacterial content during a time when people knew little of commercial pasteurization. Mrs. White also had negative comments about butter, because at the time it was "full of germs" (3SM 221). Even then she never considered the eating of butter or cheese a sin. "The question whether we shall eat butter, meat, or cheese is not to be presented to anyone as a test." "Tea, coffee, tobacco, and alcohol we must present as sinful indulgences. We cannot place on the same ground [that is, as a sinful indulgence] meat, eggs, butter, cheese, and such articles placed upon the table. . . . The poisonous narcotics are not to be treated in the same way as the subject of eggs, butter, and cheese" (ibid. 287).

But outside the bacterial considerations we find that a prudent application of these two opposite counsels will guide us into a more healthful approach to the use of cheese. We should never consider it as wrong in the eyes of God to eat it. However, medical science has proven that because of its high fat content, too much of it can be a major factor in clogging the arteries. If we eat such products, it should be in moderation.

When I heard the woman's comment about cheese, I knew she had adopted a strong position against it. I also realized that if I took some, she would probably notice it and possibly have different feelings toward my preaching to her about the love of Jesus. Just then, in my mind, the Holy Spirit asked me the question: "Do you love your appetite more than your fellow Christian?" Trying to be honest with God, I mentally replied, "Yes, I do." Then He asked me, "Keavin, what would Jesus do?"

Remembering that people are more important than food, I joined Daniel's band and "purposed in my heart not to defile myself with the king's meat." So I closed my eyes, held my breath, and quickly bypassed that pan of lasagna. As my eyes opened they fell upon my consolation prize, a big bowl of peas and carrots. But what was more intriguing to me was the gentle touch of a hand on my arm. As I turned, I saw her little smiling face. To this day her words still echo in my ears. "I see you don't eat cheese either!" At that moment I wanted nothing more than to give her a straight testimony, so with a smile I returned, "My dear sister, I wouldn't condemn anyone if they did."

I would like to pause here to define a point that could easily get confused in our thinking. I have often stated in this book that the principle of golden rule living requires that we be sensitive to the positions of others and to try our best not to cause them to stumble. But we can go overboard even with this principle. Peter used the argument that he didn't want to upset his fellow Israelites by dining with Gentiles, but Paul rebuked him anyway (see Gal. 2:11-14). Often traditional Adventism uses this argument as a strategy to keep things the way they like it, thus failing to take into consideration the needs of those who need something different (i.e., accommodating young people's choice of music or reaching out to meet evangelistic interests at their level). This of course stifles the true spirit of evangelism.

My story about the woman and the cheese could have just as easily turned out the opposite way. Sometimes Adventist minds that are cemented into extremism need to be blasted out with a radical witness of that which might offend them. If I had felt the Lord directing me to do so, I would have taken the cheese in front of her. It is a matter of how we perceive the Lord to be impressing our conscience. There is no one set policy to follow for every instance.

Extremist minds need to learn that the real purpose of health reform is not as a means to salvation but rather to help us have clear minds and to make our Christian witness more effective. Ellen White appropriately identified it as the right arm of the message we have to give to the world (CH 434). However, please notice that it is not the message itself but that it simply opens doors to deliver the true message—the third angel's message. And that message is not about what you eat, but about the saving power of Jesus Christ experienced in the life by faith.

The ultimate focus of our health message should be the teaching of glorification. It is a worthy thing to be involved in the betterment of people's lives here and now. But get them off the drugs, the alcohol, the tobacco, the caffeine, the meat, the sugar, the junk food, add a few years to their lives down here, and guess what—as with the cases of Hezekiah and Namaan, whom God healed, they too will eventually die anyway! Sure, they will have a better quality of life while living, but isn't the ultimate goal an eternal bill of health?

I thought a pastor friend of mine did a beautiful job of sharing this concept with a cancer victim we visited recently. She had requested anointing, and we went to her home to perform the service. The pastor quoted James 5:15: "And the prayer of faith shall save the sick, and the Lord shall raise him up; and if he have committed sins, they shall be forgiven him." Then, taking hold of the cancerous and swollen hand, he explained to her that real healing first takes place in our hearts through knowing that Christ has forgiven us. Thus we become joint heirs with Him in eternal life. Next, he promised her that if she believed in Jesus as her personal Saviour, her healing was guaranteed. Yet its timing was up to God. He might choose to heal her immediately. Possibly He might heal her over time through medical treatment and/or lifestyle changes. Or He might choose to wait until the resurrection. His point was that healing was not a matter of *if,* but *when.* When we reach the place where Jesus is real to us and becomes the focal point of our hope, how can we lose?

The reality is that we are all in the dying process because we are sick with the cancer of sin. The healing of our soul begins only as we accept Jesus as our Saviour and the forgiveness He has for us. But our ultimate healing doesn't come until glorification. This should be the pinnacle of our health message—not just the temporary benefits, but the eternal rewards that we receive only through a personal faith in Christ. The health message, when rightly employed, will open doors for us to share this good news!

## *Practical Applications*

The health counsels we have received through the pen of Ellen White are wonderful. If followed they will bring us a greater degree of spiritual discernment. However, to a large extent the living conditions and general lack of public knowledge in the area of health that Ellen White wrote about are no longer a real issue in modern nations such as America. In her day people lived without proper sanitation, thought tobacco smoke was a cure for lung diseases, believed that certain fresh fruits and vegetables such as tomatoes were poisonous, and even feared ventilation in their houses because they considered fresh air to be dangerous. Today we have been blessed with such devices as septic and ventilation systems. An increase in understanding disease (the knowledge of germs was just beginning in Ellen White's day) and nutrition (they didn't know what a vitamin was, either) has brought tremendous changes in the general public's view of healthful living. Now we have the privilege of traveling in smoke-free environments and a year-round selection of fresh produce as well as an array of other healthy food choices from around the world.

Without doubt what Ellen White advocated in the area of health has withstood the test of time and modern science. To a great degree the lifestyle habits now promoted by the world's leading health experts increasingly echo what she wrote nearly 100 years ago in her classic work *The Ministry of Healing:* "Pure air, sunlight, abstemiousness, rest, exercise, proper diet, the use of water, trust in divine power—these are the true remedies. Every person should have a knowledge of nature's remedial agencies and how to apply them" (MH 127).

Let us now take a brief look at these eight guides for securing better health.

## *Guide One—Nutrition*

In 1977 the United States Senate issued a report entitled "Dietary Goals for the United States." It was the first comprehensive statement by the federal government regarding risk factors in the American diet. Senator George McGovern, chairman of the Select Committee on Nutrition and Human Needs (the committee that issued the report), stated in a press conference on January 14, 1977: "The simple fact is that our diets have changed radically within the last 50 years, with great and often very harmful effects on our health. These dietary changes represent as great a threat to public health as smoking. Too much fat, too much sugar and salt, can be and are linked directly to heart disease, cancer, obesity, and stroke, among other killer diseases. In all, six of the ten leading causes of death in the United States have been linked to our diet."

Even though this report framed its findings in the negative, by acting upon its warnings we can reap positive results of better health. The key to nourishing the body properly is to provide it with those food elements needed to make good blood and other cells, while at the same time choosing not to use things that will hinder the natural operation of the human system.

Most of us make our dietary choices based upon what appeals to our taste buds, cravings that have in most cases been perverted by habits we acquired early in life. So to benefit our health, we must intelligently choose those foods that are best for us. Altering our food choices, along with modifying our eating habits, is a continuous task. It will be difficult at times to train our taste buds away from the poor food choices we have become accustomed to and replace them with more natural, wholesome foods. But once they are adjusted, we will come to relish those natural foods with greater enjoyment than we ever did the more processed ones.

The various dietary counsels, considered in the context in which Ellen White gave them, provide us a goal to use in the work of reshaping our diets. Remember, we cannot accomplish it overnight, but we can keep striving for it. The closer we bring our life habits into harmony with these dietary goals, the greater health benefits we will actually experience.

## Guide Two—Exercise

Daily exercise is an absolute necessity to good health. Because people are more sedentary today than in the agrarian society of Ellen White's time, perhaps we need her counsel about exercise even more. For most of us exercise will not be a part of our daily work routine, so we will have to make special effort to get it. I have noticed that many who harp on restricting the diet often fail to get adequate exercise. In some cases, exercise may be a greater factor for improved health than restricting or modifying diet.

How much better would many who now complain of sickness feel if they would simply venture outdoors each day for just 30 minutes of aerobic exercise. A fast walk, head and shoulders lifted and arms swinging, is all it takes. It will increase blood circulation, bringing needed supplies of fresh oxygen to the lungs and body cells, new life to the muscles, and clearness of thought to the brain. Routine exercise will prove a soothing relaxant to troubled and tensed nerves and will make our mental outlook brighter.

Those who feel the need for more strenuous exertion have a

wide choice of activities available. Gardening or other forms of lighter exercise will provide most with all the exertion they require. As usual, each should individually determine what their real needs are.

## Guide Three—Water

O ur bodies consist of more than 75 percent water. The average adult loses approximately 64 ounces of water a day, which we need to replace in order to keep the body healthy. The body works best with pure water. When water is obtained through manufactured beverages, the body must first filter the water before it can use it.

The internal use of water is essential, because it bathes the cells, thus aiding the body in ridding itself of impurities. It also keeps the body temperature regulated and lubricates the entire system.

The external application of water to our bodies is one of the easiest ways to regulate blood circulation. Foot baths, fomentations, and steam baths assist the body in recovering from a number of ailments. And that simple daily bath or shower will not only rid the skin of the impurities put out daily through its pores, but will relax our nerves and rejuvenate our brains.

Because of polluted water sources, we must be careful that the water we drink is safe.

## Guide Four—Sunshine

S unshine provides several benefits to the body. The sun is our best source for natural vitamin D, a substance that helps the body assimilate calcium and supplies it with energy.

It also soothes the nerves. A daily moderate dose of sunshine (10 to 15 minutes on each side of the face without burning), even in winter, will help boost the immune system to fight off colds and give the skin a healthy appearance. Today, though, because of the shrinking ozone layer, we must not overexpose ourselves, and we should avoid sunburn because of the increasing risk of skin cancer.

## Guide Five—Temperance

Temperance is the moderate use of those things that are good for us and rejecting those things that have proven to be harmful. Ellen White placed dangerous drugs, alcohol, tobacco, and caffeinated beverages in the category of things to avoid. In addition, we should practice moderation in the areas of work, sex, rest, exercise, or anything else we do on a regular basis.

## Guide Six—Fresh Air

The greatest need of the body is pure air. Every cell of the body needs oxygen. Even better, it doesn't cost anything. The purest form of air is the outdoor air found in an unpolluted environment free from tobacco smoke and smog. If we are indoors, fresh air entering through open windows will invigorate us. Proper posture and outdoor exercise daily will help ensure that we get enough oxygen to our bodies.

## Guide Seven—Rest

The body will not function properly without adequate sleep. While we sleep the body cleanses itself, repairs and rebuilds its cells, and regains energy for the next day's activities. The brain also is quite active processing and storing information, activity that if not completed during sleep will seriously damage our ability to function during waking hours. The body's regeneration is best accomplished when the body receives regular sleeping hours. Research estimates that the average person spends one third of their life sleeping. How careful should we be, then, that our sleep is of the best quality possible. If we are following all the other guides to better health, good sound sleep will be more automatic.

Also, in the evening, the body's digestive organs will have finished their daily tasks and are themselves ready for a period of rest. Supper, if taken at all, is of a lighter fare. The old saying always proves true—"Breakfast is gold, dinner is silver, and supper is lead!" A large complex meal in the evening tends to disturb good sound sleep, because the digestive organs have to keep working while the other parts of our body rest. A light meal in the evening, though it takes some getting used to, will always result in a noticeable improvement in the way one feels when waking the following day.

A relaxing bath just before bedtime, along with fresh air during the night, will also aid in achieving the best quality of sleep.

## Guide Eight—Trust in Divine Power

Positive thinking is the best medicine available. The Bible says: "A merry heart does good like medicine, but a broken spirit dries the bones" (Prov. 17:22, NKJV). Without question, the best way to think positively is to fix the mind upon God's loving character. Watching television programs and listening to music that promote such things as loveless sex, drugs, violence, and infidelity are destroying the mental happiness of millions. Replacing such habits with a daily routine of enjoying the positive things of life—exploring nature, spending quality time with the ones we love, learning creativity through simple, unselfish, and practical ways—will go a long way toward maintaining our own happiness. Coupled with this, setting aside some time each day for communion with God through personal prayer, meditation, and Bible study will ensure us a longer and better quality life. The knowledge that God loves and accepts us, forgives our past sins, and is providentially laboring for our best interests is the answer to all our life's troubles. To know that we are living in a way that pleases Him will prove the best defense against disease, both mental and physical.

We acquire wrong habits of living through years and years of repetition. To change such poor practices for the ones we have discussed is not easy. "With men this is impossible; but with God all things are possible" (Matt. 19:26). The Lord truly wants us to have not only eternal life but also the best quality of life possible during our stay here on earth. He is totally committed to helping us better our existence. If we truly believe this, and learn to rely on His divine power to assist us in our efforts to change our life habits, we can be assured of achieving and maintaining optimum health.

*Chapter Nine*
# Principles of Association

E schatology has always played a big part in determining how Adventists live. In fact, our denomination received its foundations from a religious movement (the Millerites) motivated by the belief that the time for the end of the world had come in 1844. Ever since, one of the most difficult things for Adventists has been to establish a balanced view on how to associate with the world in which they live. A "time of trouble" mentality erodes away at our church like the relentless waves of the ocean. News of world events or statements by world religious leaders affects Adventism as financial indicators from the Federal Reserve Board influence the stock market. Because of our knowledge of certain end-time prophecies we seem unable to escape speculation on anything that appears to point to their fulfillment.

For example, Adventists in the 1860s thought the American Civil War might lead to the end of the world, little realizing that the world was much bigger than their young America. World War I raised the fears of church members in that day because of its more global nature. World War II only intensified Adventists' expectations of the end as they daily read headlines of Hitler's apparent success in reunifying Europe. Then came the cold war years, along with their danger of nuclear annihilation. And more recently the rise of millennial fever brought its concerns about Y2K and how it might bring everything to an end. Not to mention the fanatical elements among us who from time to time try to predict the dates on which certain end-time events will take place.

I know of cases in which church building committees have constructed cheaply because they anticipated not needing the building for more than 20 or 30 years. They were certain that Jesus would come before then. In subsequent years their congregations spent as much maintaining the ill-devised structure as it would have cost to have done it right the first time. The result was a building that year by year depreciated in real estate value while the congregation needed a better facility.

I have seen parents who made little or no planning for their children's future, or even their own retirement, because they never thought it would come to that point. By the time they discovered they were wrong they had wasted years, cheated their children of educational opportunities, and themselves faced financial difficulty in their old age.

No one would question the sincerity of those who have lost interest in living in this present world of sin and suffering, especially in the light of eternity. Anyone who understands the Bible's message for the last days will certainly have their affections weaned from earth. "They desire a better country, that is, an heavenly" (Heb. 11:16). But in light of how God wants us to live in a world of apocalyptic threats, it is vitally important that we learn to live balanced lives in relation to such signs of the times.

While we want to remain sensitive and alert to the fulfillment of biblical prophecy, at the same time we must guard against jumping to unwarranted conclusions by reading something apocalyptic into every little piece of news. Failure to do so always injures God's cause as well as weakens our own faith. *A religion of extremes can be very intoxicating, confusing our senses and disorienting our common sense.* Fear and self preservation drive it. Living under a "time of trouble" mentality can never produce the kind of healthy, balanced witness that will bring glory to Christ's cause on earth.

So how do we do it? How do we exist from day to day despite our knowledge of what the future holds for our planet? Actually, it was to this end that Jesus prayed for us as He wound up His pilgrimage here. "I pray not that thou shouldest take them out of the world, but that thou shouldest keep them from the evil. . . . As thou hast sent me into the world, even so have I also sent them into the world" (John 17:15-18). Here we have our first clue. Jesus doesn't want us to isolate ourselves from the society around us. Rather, He desires that we mingle with people as a "witness unto all nations; and then shall the end come" (Matt. 24:14). Notice that the end doesn't come until the job of witnessing is done! And how are we going to be a witness from our time-of-trouble hide-outs in the wilderness?

"But," some say, "we will get tainted with evil if we mingle with society." May we ever remember that Joseph stood in Egypt and Daniel in Babylon, but Adam fell in Paradise! The determining factor of our spiritual stability is not where our physical presence is, but where we center our thoughts. Here is the secret to winning the battle—to keep our mind riveted on God in the midst of our surroundings. We have the promise "Thou wilt keep him in perfect peace, whose mind is stayed on thee: because he trusteth in thee" (Isa. 26:3). If we are careful to anchor our minds deep in the gospel reality that our hope for eternal security comes from trusting in Christ's grace, separate from our earthly circumstances and surroundings, then it frees us to labor among unsaved elements with perfect peace and remain spiritually unaffected.

No doubt that was why Daniel made it a practice to pray three times a day in the polytheistic culture of the Medes and Persians. Because he maintained his connection with Christ, God protected him even in the midst of devouring lions. And Joseph was able to remain true to God's commandments only as he had assurance of his salvation. Speaking of those who maintain such faith, Jesus said that they would be enabled to tread upon serpents and remain unaffected (Luke 10:19). If you consider the spiritual meaning of serpents as representing fallen angels, it gives insight into just how powerful an effect the gospel can have over one's mind. Not that we should seek to become spiritual snake handlers by purposefully seeking out the companionship of demons, but we can have the assurance of God's sustaining grace when He calls us to leave our comfort zone to seek those lost in sin.

God will answer Christ's prayer and keep us from evil even in the midst of some very evil environments. But that is only possible as we have a good grasp of the gospel of salvation through the gift of Christ's grace alone. If we have a legalistic fixation on external behavior, then we will flee because of a fear of being corrupted in the very places where God desires we witness. Such self-righteousness and self-preservation go hand in hand, and like the Pharisees we will begin to look suspiciously upon anyone who gets close "with publicans and sinners" (Mark 2:16).

Of course we should not purposely place ourselves in covenant-type relationships with those whose influence will wear down our Christian commitment. That is why God warns us not to marry un-believers or form business partnerships with them. It goes beyond the limits that the Lord has placed in His Word for our protection. "No one who fears God can without danger connect himself with one who fears Him not. 'Can two walk together, except they be agreed?' (Amos 3:3). The happiness and prosperity of the marriage relation depends upon the unity of the parties; but between the be-liever and the unbeliever there is a radical difference of tastes, incli-nations, and purposes. They are serving two masters, between whom there can be no concord. However pure and correct one's principles may be, the influence of an unbelieving companion will have a tendency to lead away from God. . . . The Lord's direction is 'Be ye not unequally yoked together with unbelievers' (2 Cor. 6:14, 17, 18)" (CC 57; see also HS 215 regarding unsanctified business partnerships). However, we must point out that "those who enter the marriage relation while unconverted should not after conversion leave their unbelieving companions" (ST, Apr. 10, 1879).

## Effective Witnessing

A consistent Christian witness is possible only for mature Christians. While they hold true to Bible standards as a basic guide for how to live, they will in no way come across as condemning those around them who do not share their convictions. They will accept other people for who they are and where they are at. Not only will they not judge them, even in their thoughts, but they will constantly look for avenues to share with them the faith they have in Christ as the only hope for salvation. Such individuals will follow the example of Daniel, who, while he determined in his heart not to defile himself with the king's food, also said to Nebuchadnezar, "O king, live forever." By accepting the Babylonians where they were, and through witnessing to a better way of life, Daniel let God use him to bring the king of Babylon into a saving re-lationship with the King of kings!

Jesus employed the same formula for witnessing. While He per-sonally held to the highest standards of living, people who didn't share them still felt comfortable in His presence. They didn't feel condemned by Him, but rather loved and accepted. Though some of the pious priests looked down upon and rejected them, in the very countenance of Jesus they read, "Neither do I condemn thee" (John 8:11; cf. 3:17). His loving example and accepting spirit created within them a desire to do right and led them to genuine repentance. He has told us that only by following His example of Christian witnessing will we know true success in our soul-winning endeavors. "Christ's method alone will give true success in reaching the people. *The Saviour mingled with men* as one who desired their good. He showed His sympathy for them, ministered to their needs, and won their confidence. Then He bade them, 'Follow Me.' *There is need of coming close to the people by personal effort*" (MH 143; italics supplied).

My wife, Lisa, and I experienced this powerful method of soul winning recently during a series of evangelistic meetings we were holding. A woman named Jody attended the first four nights with great interest. Then, to our disappointment, she missed three meetings in a row. With concern we searched our registration cards, only to find that Jody had not disclosed her address or phone number. We had no way of contacting her. All we could do was pray that the Lord would impress her to return.

On the eighth night, just before the meeting started, my wife walked into the bathroom at the church. As she opened the door, there stood Jody. Lisa was so excited that she immediately threw out her arms to embrace her with a hug. But Jody somehow resisted the hug and quickly exited the bathroom for the sanctuary.

When the meeting ended, Jody came to Lisa and apologized for rebuffing her display of affection. Jody explained it wasn't that she didn't want to be hugged, but she was embarrassed that she had just smoked a cigarette before the meeting and didn't want her to smell it. Now, Lisa could have given her a lecture on why smoking was bad for her health, but she didn't. Instead her reply was "Jody, I don't care if you smoked 10 cigarettes before you came; I'm just glad and excited that you are here." What's more important, it was not just some canned response my wife had learned to give. She actually meant what she said, and Jody knew it was genuine.

Jody continued to attend the meetings faithfully and within a week the woman came privately to Lisa and requested prayer. She said she was attempting to stop smoking and knew she needed the Lord's help. What was so powerful about this experience is that no one had said a word about her smoking—except the Holy Spirit. I had not said a word about it from the platform, and Lisa did not condemn her when she found out that she smoked. But when she decided to quit, it was Lisa she turned to for support. Jody knew that she already had found acceptance in her eyes.

## Exceptions to the Rules

Maybe this would be a good time once again to place our keeping of standards in the right perspective to the gospel. We do not incorporate biblical standards into our life to obtain salvation. Jesus grants salvation to us the moment we accept Him as our perfect Substitute—before we even begin to make any outward changes.

There should be two main purposes for living Christian standards. One is to exalt God by demonstrating the power of His gospel in enabling us to live changed lives. The other is to meet others at their hurting points and give them hope to continue living. Jesus said that to live in such a way is to truly demonstrate what it means to keep His law (see Matthew 22:36-40). He also summed up the witnessing value of golden rule living when He said: "Let your light so shine before men, that they may see your good works, and glorify your Father which is in heaven" (Matt. 5:16).

But we mar God's beautiful design to reach others when we deliberately transgress one of His commandments, or we set the standards higher than God ever intended them. It is vitally important that we stay close to a heart commitment to God and allow His law to guide our lives. If King David had done this, he would have been able to bypass the saddest chapter of his life, his adulterous affair with Bathsheba and the murder of her husband. His story records that even those truly seeking God with their whole heart are not immune to sin.

On the other hand, we also face the danger of becoming like the Pharisees when we set the standard higher than even God does. Their standards regarding Sabbath observance made even Jesus appear as a liberal commandment breaker. We too can fall into the trap of becoming overconscientious and creating for ourselves an unreal world of holy living that few people will ever be able to relate to. As the old saying tries to point out: "We can become so heavenly minded that we are of no earthly good." God set the principles behind the commandments in stone. It is their interpretation and application that we need to watch, lest we overshoot God's intentions.

God has given warnings in His Word to safeguard us in our human weaknesses. Though He has not called us to a life of monasticism or spiritual seclusion, there are occasions that it would be healthy and wise for us to consider.

To begin with, sometimes we do need "wilderness experiences." The Bible tells us that even those who possessed the strongest faith still needed to get away from it all and find uninterrupted time and space with God. Moses discovered God in the Midian desert; Elijah was refreshed alone with God by the brook Cherith; John the Baptist grew up unaffected by worldly influences in the Judean wilderness; and the young convert Saul of Tarsus needed a few years' seclusion in Arabia (modern-day Jordan) to get it all straightened out before he began his commission of evangelizing the Gentile world. Even Jesus, after His baptism, had the Spirit lead Him into a 40-day retreat during which He could be alone with His Father to seriously contemplate His lifework.

I can promise you that we are no different. If giants of faith required a wilderness experience with God, then how do we think we can make it without it? Some circumstances, especially with those young in the faith, demand that people withdraw themselves as much as possible from the influence of society and seek God alone.

## A Personal Experience

I was 25 years old when I had my first wilderness experience with God. Two years earlier I had graduated from college and had begun a career in pharmaceutical sales. My goal in life was to be successful in business, make lots of money, and enjoy all the material benefits that such a life afforded. Then I met Jesus and was converted that day in western Tennessee.

After my conversion, I, along with my wife, began to look at life differently. The career, the money, the nice cars, and the fancy homes had no real appeal to us anymore. In fact, trying to keep up with society's standards now seemed to us like a rat race, with everyone trying to acquire the most cheese. We didn't want the cheese anymore—we just wanted out of the trap.

What's more, while I knew about a lot of things, I was, for all practical purposes, ignorant about what now meant the most to me—God. I could recite sports trivia, was well informed concerning the latest movies, could identify the recording artist of nearly every song I heard on the radio, had a good background in my business, but knew virtually nothing about the kingdom of God.

Slowly but surely I began to lose so much interest in those things that intrigue the world that I began to withdraw myself from them. Then, in the spring of 1986, it happened. I resigned from my job, and my wife and I sold our new home, cars, and nearly all our home furnishings. What remained we loaded into the trunk of an older model car and drove off to a secluded country farmhouse we had rented in western Kentucky.

Needless to say, business acquaintances, friends, neighbors, family members, and even church members nearly all thought we had gone off the deep end of religious extremism. Well, from their perspective they were right. But for us it was like a giant sigh of relief. That summer there in the country, without a phone or television, we had one of the most awesome experiences of our lifetime. With no worries about trying to keep up with society's pace we spent those summer days together gardening, enjoying nature, and praying. More important, we had the opportunity to spend undivided time with God through the study of His Word.

After about a year the Lord began to impress us with the need to go back to work and be a part of modern society. That we did, yet our experience in the country remains etched upon our minds. We had gone through the experience of giving up everything and knew that if God ever called us to do it again, we could and would.

After getting involved again in the "real world," settling into a new job, and establishing a new home, I went through the struggle of wondering if we had been irrational in our decision to give it all up the year before. We had a lot of catching up to do, especially financially. Echoes of what people had said concerning the extremity of what we had done continued to ring through my head. *Maybe they were right,* I thought. *Maybe I was just overcome by a fever of religious fanaticism.*

One day I shared my experience with a new friend and told him of the discouraging thoughts I had been having about it all. His analysis was truly like "apples of gold in pictures of silver." He explained that rockets have extremely powerful engines because of the enormous amount of energy it requires to get them out of the earth's atmosphere. But after the vehicle clears the earth's gravity the engines cut back and the astronauts begin focusing on leveling the ship out to an orbital speed.

The experience of a new Christian is often very similar, he said. By the time most of us find Christ we are so deeply entrenched in the gravitational pull of our world's society that it requires a great amount of spiritual energy to break us out of its atmosphere. But once we accomplish that by the power of the gospel, we can balance out and live a practical life for Christ even in the midst of a world of sin. Often it requires a wilderness experience with God. That time of separation from the things that naturally pull us back into our old ways of thinking and living helps us come to grips with the ramifications of what it really means to be a Christian in this life.

Now, in no way am I trying to prescribe for everyone the experience that my wife and I went through. We are convinced, though, that God saw that's what we needed. It was our personal experience. What I am suggesting is that we each be honest with how our present society affects us spiritually, and then prayerfully decide and act accordingly as to how limited we need to be in our association with it. We may not take an entire year off. It may require only a few days, weeks, or months to get our priorities realigned. God will lead each to just the experience they need.

## A Friend of the World?

The Bible is clear that "whosoever therefore will be a friend of the world is the enemy of God" (James 4:4). Paul instructs us that in "denying ungodliness and worldly lusts, we should live soberly, righteously, and godly, in this present world" (Titus 2:12). And Jesus taught that it would be better for us to pluck out our eye or cut off our hand than to tolerate an association with anything or anybody that would sever our eternal relationship with Him (Matt. 5:29, 30).

Another key in remaining unaffected by the world's influence is to control our thinking. All outward manifestations of sin have their beginning in the thoughts. That's why Paul spoke of the importance of "bringing into captivity every thought to the obedience of Christ" (2 Cor. 10:5). James suggests that outward sins begin with lustful thoughts. Then when such lust conceives it will eventually give birth to sin and spiritual death (James 1:14, 15). Of course, the godly thing to do in such a scenario is to abort the thought before it develops into deed. Though it requires a struggle to train the mind to do it, with the Spirit's help it can be done.

But as we consider these strong counsels against worldliness, we must remember several things. First, different things affect different people in different ways. What may threaten one person's eternal commitment may not hold the same dangers for another. That is why we must learn to know ourselves and then evaluate what standards we need without requiring the exact same thing from everyone else.

For example, Ellen White had quite a bit to say about leaving large cities and moving out to the country. While her counsel is quite appropriate for some, to others it does not necessarily apply. People addicted to metropolitan living, or who have young children to raise, would probably be wise in carefully planning an exodus from such a society and reap the benefits that country living has to offer. But if every Adventist exited the cities, how would God's work be accomplished in the very places where a major part of the earth's population dwells? In the United States White Adventists have given up on the cities. Adventist churches in major urban areas consist almost entirely of minorities. But elsewhere in the world large numbers of church members live in the city. Some major cities in South America, for example, have church memberships in the tens of thousands.

Millions of God's representatives labor amid such environments and yet continue to grow spiritually. Such individuals are qualified to answer the Lord's call to evangelize the cities by saying "Here am I, Lord; send me."

Which brings us to our second point. In telling us not to be a friend of the world God is not forbidding us to befriend the world.

He has commissioned us to mingle with the unsaved, not to adopt their attitudes and desires, but to gain their confidence and lead them to accept the eternal life that only Jesus Christ can offer them. Never should we be in their presence without Christ and His commission on our mind.

It's like the man who first shared with me the three angels' messages. Shortly after our baptism my wife and I visited the home of her Catholic parents. It was a Friday night, and we had just finished sundown worship. Just then my father-in-law came into the living room. He was discouraged because none of his Catholic relatives would go with him to a Christmas concert and Mass. Before I knew it I had offered to go with him, and we were in his car racing to make it to the church on time. Being a new Adventist, I was unsure as to how God looked upon my going to a Catholic Mass and musical production during the Sabbath hours. My concept of Sabbath observance at that time was pretty rigid, so I spent most of the time during the service in a repentant state of mind for being there. I was trying my best not to allow my supposed holy state of being to become infected by the worldly influences around me or by the evil angels that I imagined were floating just below the cathedral ceiling that evening.

Afterward people began to socialize with each other, and I felt like a fish out of water. Then, to my absolute surprise and holy horror, I looked across the room and saw the Adventist man who had brought me into the church. *What is he doing here?* I thought to myself. *Doesn't he have any regard for God's holy Sabbath day?* I marched right over to him and said, "Bill, what are you doing here?"

"Shhhhhh," he replied. Then, opening up his long winter overcoat, he revealed to me an arsenal of *Steps to Christ* and *The Desire of Ages* and said, "These precious Catholics are some of the most spiritually interested people in town!"

Oh, to be able to labor for the Lord in a balanced way has to be the most pleasing thing in God's sight. Yes, it requires spiritual maturity, but this will come to everyone who places themselves in the school of Christ. "Ye are the salt of the earth," Jesus said, "but if the salt have lost his savour, wherewith shall it be salted? it is thenceforth good for nothing, but to be cast out, and to be trodden under foot of men" (Matt. 5:13). "Ye are my witnesses, saith the

Lord, and my servant whom I have chosen" (Isa. 43:10).

May God grant us the spiritual maturity and courage we need to become the effective witnesses that He has called us to be. May He give us wisdom to determine just what degree of association we are to have with the world around us as we come closer and closer to the great event of His advent.

One thing is certain—how we relate to all this end-time stuff will determine our effectiveness as witnesses. God's remnant of witnesses will realize that even though Jesus said, "Be ye also ready" (Matt. 24:44), He also said, "Occupy till I come" (Luke 19:13). This will be the secret to their balancing act. Though they carry on with life in a responsible way, providing for their families through hard work and wise investments, they will be ready to give it all up when it truly comes time to go home or when God's cause on earth requires it of them.

## Chapter Ten

# The Two Adventisms

I n the area of lifestyle issues, differing philosophical positions constantly swirl beneath the surface of Adventism. As time advances, these differences will more and more emerge to the forefront. Two classes, one tending toward conservatism, the other toward more liberal opinions, will oppose each other as to how a Seventh-day Adventist should relate to the subject. Already we see the opposition of the two manifesting itself in contentions over the role of women in the church, music, jewelry, etc.

The definition of the terms *conservative* and *liberal* are as varied as the people who define them. In both camps we find degrees of opinion all along the scale. For example, I know some conservatives who consider anyone liberal who thinks it's OK for women to wear pants or slacks. On the other hand, I know women who wear pants who would classify themselves as conservative.

I think it safe to say that as a whole the general Christian world would classify Adventists as a conservative group. Few among our ranks would knowingly espouse the real liberal theological views engulfing modern Christianity, such as denying the virgin birth, rejecting the substitutionary atonement for salvation, or questioning the authenticity of Christ's miracles.

To a great degree, most in our church find themselves defined as liberals or conservatives mainly on how they personally relate to lifestyle practices. Even then, most other Christians would still look upon Adventists as conservative. As I wrote this book I often wondered what a Baptist or Catholic would think as they read about our century-old debate on whether or not it is a sin to eat cheese! Or that some Adventist pastors are still reluctant to consider baptism for anyone who wears a wedding ring. We Adventists are so used to living in our little subculture that we define the terms *conservative* or *liberal* by what is going on in our own microcosm.

## Dangers and Pitfalls

For the sake of identifying with the majority of my readers, let's work within the Adventist realm of definition. It is not safe to accept or reject a position on an issue just because it comes from one group or the other. Both the conservative and liberal camps have dangers and pitfalls that we must avoid.

Liberal attitudes are positive in the sense that they are more open to grant others the right to express what they believe. They do not conform as much to tradition just for the sake of tradition, but are willing to investigate new ideas. This of course encourages the mind to expand and be creative as it seeks to become an effective witness for Christ on earth.

However, liberalism becomes dangerous when it throws off the restraints of God's Word just because it perceives them as restricting one's freedom in Christ. The apostle Paul met this problem head-on when he warned the Galatians to "use not liberty for an occasion to the flesh" (Gal. 5:13). In other words, appreciate and enjoy the benefits of God's covering grace but don't capitalize on that grace by turning it into a presumptuous license for sinful indulgence (see Jude 4).

On the other hand, so-called conservatism also has its strengths and weaknesses. Conservatism is positive as it seeks to guard the authentic Bible truths established by those who have gone before us. It also provides a safer environment for those who tend to get out of control with the freedom that Christ's grace offers. Those just coming into the church from a life of sinful living will find security in the restraining influence of conservative Adventism. The Adventist lifestyle aids them in putting their moral lives back together.

But conservatism ceases to be helpful when it begins to spend more time defending the old than discovering the new. It is more apt to slip into the false security of Laodiceanism, deceiving people into feeling that they are "rich, and increased with goods, and have need of nothing" (Rev. 3:17) when the reality is that they are being left behind by the advancing march of truth.

Though conservatism has many wonderful safeguards built into its philosophy, once again, it can be a subtle enemy to true spiritual growth. Ellen White foresaw the danger when she warned: "Many give the words of Scripture a meaning that suits their own opinions, and they mislead themselves and deceive others by their misinterpretations of God's Word. . . . Long-cherished opinions must not be regarded as infallible. It was the unwillingness of the Jews to give up their long-established traditions that proved their ruin. They were determined not to see any flaw in their own opinions or in their expositions of the Scriptures; but however long men may have entertained certain views, if they are not clearly sustained by the written word, they should be discarded" (CW 36, 37). "As real spiritual life declines, it has ever been the tendency to cease to advance in the knowledge of the truth. Men rest satisfied with the light already received from God's Word, and discourage any further investigation of the Scriptures. *They become conservative,* and seek to avoid discussion. . . . There is reason to fear that they may not be clearly discriminating between truth and error. When no new questions are started by investigation of the Scriptures, when no difference of opinion arises which will set men to searching the Bible for themselves, to make sure that they have the truth, there will be many now, as in ancient times, who will hold to tradition, and worship they know not what" (*ibid.* 39; italics supplied).

It is never safe to rely on only what human beings, whether they be liberal or conservative, say is truth. I meet some who are inclined to accept something as truth just because a popular minister said it. "I like Pastor So and so, and Pastor So and so says" can often be heard in Adventist circles. Now, I know most ministers would agree with me when I say it is not safe to base a conviction on a "thus saith" any person. With all due respect to the ministers of our or any other denomination, they are fallible just like the rest of us.

It's all right to listen to people who minister in the public forum. But we had better get to studying ourselves. With all due respect to Adventist media ministries, the advent of Adventist television has begun to create a population of Adventist couch potatoes. Though such ministries provide a wonderful service to those who cannot attend church, we should never consider them an authority for truth or a substitute for personal study. Many watch a presentation on television and consider it an undisputable Bible study on the basis that a certain minister taught it. While we certainly can learn by listening to what others have to say, we do not know what real Bible study is until we take a Bible in one hand and a concordance in the other, get away from all our preconceived opinions, fall on our knees asking the living God to reveal truth to us, and then read everything the Bible has to say about the topic under consideration. Until we do this for ourselves we are not on safe ground. The Lord's purpose in public Christian ministries is to stimulate our thinking—not to do it for us.

## Identifying With Others

I personally do not wish to be classified or stereotyped as either a conservative or liberal Christian. What I desire to be is a commonsense Christian, identifying myself with both groups on points that line up with Scripture. I want to experience the saving power of the gospel on the basis of Christ's merits alone, apart from my efforts to live a holy lifestyle. Yet I don't want to involve myself in any practice that would cause others to stumble or that would otherwise dishonor my Lord or deny my professed faith. I want to hang on to those traditional teachings and practices of our past that we can clearly substantiate from the Word of God. However, I also want to remain flexible enough to change my position once I realize that my present understanding rests more on Adventist traditionalism than on the Bible. I desire to become more active in reaching the unsaved for Christ, even though I may have to move out of my comfort zone in order to identify with them.

The Lord taught me this lesson one evening while on a plane from Chicago to Grand Rapids, Michigan. A nice-looking couple about my age were seated across the aisle from me. Feeling an unusual burden to witness to them, I tried to strike up a conversation. Soon I discovered they were returning home from a week's vacation at the casinos in Las Vegas.

No matter what avenue I tried, the man showed no real interest in conversing with me. I tried to introduce several topics I thought might interest him, hoping to spark a desire for conversation. But none engaged his attention. Then I asked what he did for a living. He responded that he was a disc jockey for a rock and roll radio station in southern Michigan.

Now, I grew up in the rock culture, but for 15 years I have had no real involvement in it. In fact, at that time I viewed even conversing on the topic as vain and idle talk. My conservative tendencies told me that surely the One who declared in Matthew 12:37 that my words would either justify or condemn me would not condone a discussion on the topic.

But I still felt compelled to witness to them. So I quickly prayed, "Lord, what is the key to this man's interest?" The answer came back to my mind, "Ask him what the first rock concert he ever attended was, and then share with him the experience you had at your first concert."

Now, some may wonder whether it was really God who suggested that thought to me. Let each decide that for themselves. All I know is that it worked. That man came alive and wouldn't stay quiet the entire flight. By the time we reached Grand Rapids it was as though we had known each other for years. As we landed he turned and asked, "Oh, by the way, what do you do for a living?" I responded that I was a writer and public speaker on religious and political issues shaping our world. I briefly explained to him the potential of world trouble through the uniting of the world governments and churches. He listened intently and responded that he could see the danger of what I was saying. With that the door was wide open to give him a book outlining the message of Christ's mercy that we have to give the world.

As I was waiting for my luggage at the baggage claim area, I watched him and his wife walk toward the parking lot door. He glanced over at me, and I responded by waving to him.

Then he stopped, walked over to where I was, and thanked me for what I had shared. He said that he was planning on reading the book. Needless to say, I drove home with a cheerful and grateful heart that I serve a God who is able to meet all classes of people from all walks of life. "Behold, the Lord's hand is not shortened, that it cannot save; neither his ear heavy, that it cannot hear" (Isa. 59:1).

## Redneck Christians

Last, I want to be converted and refrain from a judgmental attitude toward others because they choose to disagree with my personal convictions. (I recognize that those in leadership positions in churches, businesses, and other institutions must often make judgment calls concerning those whom they choose to work with. What I am referring to here is my personal attitude toward others in general.) I want to cease using any form of manipulation in an attempt to get others to conform to what I think they ought to do—especially as it relates to lifestyle issues. Nor do I want to make my convictions the standard for everyone else, because to do so only encourages and strengthens the spirit of antichrist within my fallen human nature. Such a course does not witness for Christ but against Him.

"Christ is the only true standard of character, and *he who sets himself up as a standard for others is putting himself in the place of Christ.* And since the Father 'hath committed all judgment unto the Son' (John 5:22), whoever presumes to judge the motives of others is again usurping the prerogative of the Son of God. *These would-be judges and critics are placing themselves on the side of antichrist,* 'who opposeth and exalteth himself above all that is called God, or that is worshiped; so that he as God sitteth in the temple of God, showing himself that he is God' (2 Thess. 2:4). . . .

"He who is guilty of wrong is the first to suspect wrong. By condemning another he is trying to conceal or excuse the evil of his own heart. It was through sin that men gained the knowledge of evil; no sooner had the first pair sinned than they began to accuse each other; and this is what human nature will inevitably do when uncontrolled by the grace of Christ.

"When men indulge this accusing spirit, they are not satisfied with pointing out what they suppose to be a defect in their brother. If milder means fail of making him do what they think ought to be done, *they will resort to compulsion.* Just as far as lies in their power *they will force men to comply with their ideas of what is right.* This is what the Jews did in the days of Christ and what the church has done ever since whenever she has lost the grace of Christ. Finding herself destitute of the power of love, she has reached out for the strong arm of the state to enforce her dogmas and execute her decrees. Here is the secret of all religious laws that have ever been enacted, and the secret of all persecution from the days of Abel to our own time.

"Christ does not drive but draws men unto Him. The only compulsion which He employs is the constraint of love. When the church begins to seek for the support of secular power, it is evident that she is devoid of the power of Christ—the constraint of divine love.

*"But the difficulty lies with the individual members of the church, and it is here that the cure must be wrought. . . .*

"If Christ is in you 'the hope of glory,' you will have no disposition to watch others, to expose their errors. Instead of seeking to accuse and condemn, it will be your object to help, to bless, and to save" (MB 125-128; italics supplied).

Here we come full circle back to the issue of religious liberty. So often we limit the concept to the enactment of Sunday laws. But it goes much deeper. The establishment of Sunday laws will be part of a larger plan to correct the moral misconduct of society. Before we ever reach the place at which we will dictate what day others should worship on, we will have had plenty of practice in judging them in regard to what they do in other areas of their life. In our minds, and often with our lips, we will have decided how they need to dress, eat, what type of music they should listen to, and all the rest. We will have nurtured a character that thinks it knows best for everybody else.

One of the most subtle dangers that stalks Adventism, it is an inescapable condition of human nature that in the end will control all, both liberal and conservative, who have not recognized and yielded to the complete lordship of Jesus Christ. It will do us no good to claim Him as our Lord when we turn around and try to be lord over others. Using modern terminology, this is nothing more than inquisition-style, redneck Christianity.

In the days of Christ a coalition between the liberal Pharisees and the conservative Sadducees sealed the Saviour's doom. He had managed to walk that fine line between the two extremes, avoiding the snares that each philosophy had set for His feet. So in our day it will be those who manage to steer clear of both the conservative and liberal ditches that the world will eventually single out as "troublers of Israel."

If we think about it for a moment we might find that the two groups are not so vastly different. On many issues both conservatives and liberals agree on what should be done. It is just that they have different ways of reaching the desired result.

I personally don't have a problem with those who choose either a conservative or more liberal lifestyle. The problem arises when either camp tries to prove that God expects what they are doing from everyone else. Though we should educate everyone to follow the principles of God's law, we must leave the specific application of those principles between the individual and God, allowing "every man to be fully persuaded in his own mind" (Rom. 14:5).

## Conclusion

In 2000 the Review and Herald Publishing Association released a book entitled *Why Our Teenagers Leave the Church.* Written by Roger L. Dudley, director of the Institute of Church Ministry at Andrews University, it offers insightful facts and conclusions based on a 10-year study tracing the lives of 1,500 Seventh-day Adventist teenagers as they grew up.

On pages 40 and 41 of his book Dudley reveals his findings on youth and church standards. His latest study paints the same picture as did the widely heralded Valuegenesis study that also monitored the convictions of Seventh-day Adventist young people concerning certain lifestyle issues. I would like to cite Dudley's findings about how our younger church members relate toward lifestyle standards.

Dudley's research evaluated our youth's opinions on 10 lifestyle issues traditionally accepted by the church. I will now list those 10 areas along with the percentages that agreed or disagreed with the church's position.

| *Lifestyle Standard* | *Percent Agree* | *Percent Disagree* |
|---|---|---|
| Not use illegal drugs | 93 | 5 |
| Not use tobacco | 92 | 4 |
| Keep the Sabbath holy | 88 | 4 |
| Not drink alcoholic beverages | 77 | 15 |
| Dress modestly | 75 | 12 |
| Sex should occur only within marriage | 74 | 14 |
| Not wear cosmetic jewelry | 33 | 49 |
| Not listen to rock music | 32 | 49 |
| Not dance | 22 | 60 |
| Not attend movie theaters | 16 | 71 |

Notice that the first six standards in the list had the support of the overwhelming majority of young people (74-93 percent for, versus 4-15 percent against). This is encouraging in that the first six standards are morally related issues. It suggests that we have been very effective at instilling moral values in our youth.

However, when it came to the last four subjects (abstaining from jewelry, rock music, dancing, and attending movie theaters), the percentages reversed (16-33 percent for, versus 49-71 percent against). Based on these findings, Dudley's conclusion is an earth-shattering one for many traditional-minded Adventists. He states: "It seems almost certain that these four standards [jewelry, rock music, dancing, and theater going] will not hold in the near future of the church" (p. 41).

Such realities are causing parents and church leaders to reevaluate where to draw the line concerning what are to be made absolute standards within the church. We have come to a fork in the road regarding our ability to obtain and retain members, particularly youth. Adventist churches all over America have become notorious for their near-empty pews scattered with a few faithful, aged, white-haired members. Through numerous studies researchers have shown us the hard facts. The results of our decisions have been unmistakably marked out for us. If we continue taking a hard-line, unbending stand regarding less morally defined issues such as jewelry, dictating to our youth what kind of music they are to listen to, and condemning their participation in such activities as dancing and theatergoing, we can expect to continue seeing them leave our church, many of them never to return. This does not mean, however, that we should stop educating them about the dangers that can occur in these four areas of lifestyle behavior.

What I'm trying to say is that an arbitrary attitude against their involvement in these areas will cause us to continue losing our young people as well as handicap our ability to bring new converts into the church. Such obstinate, judgmental attitudes against what we view as unacceptable behavior in the church will always cripple our ability to reach out to others for the Lord. Consider the story of Michal, the daughter of Saul who became King David's wife. When she saw David dancing to music in praise of the Lord, she disapproved of the low standard she felt he was setting before the people and "despised him in her heart" (2 Sam. 6:16). When David returned home that evening, Michal severely reproved him for what she considered inappropriate for any member of the church. But the Bible clearly points out that because of her stifling, condemnatory mind-set toward what she thought was offensive to God, "Michal . . . had no children to the day of her death" (verse 23). Likewise, when we think our personal convictions are the criterion by which everyone else in the church should live, we severely damage our ability to birth people into the kingdom of God.

Now, I know that to many church members this will sound like compromise. But I think we would do well to consider a few points. First, we should take into serious consideration the individual needs and choices of the differing groups that make up the church. It has always been the church's duty to minister to the various mind-sets that constitute the church and not just to one particular group. Even Ellen White saw the necessity of reaching all who were at different stages of Christian growth. Though she gave specific counsel regarding lifestyle issues, she never instructed us to push them upon people to the point at which they would leave the church. While direct and blatant violations of the commandments should always call for loving reproof, some of the more minor lifestyle issues that we have discussed in this book we should approach through educating by general principles and not by enforcing rules. One possible solution is to treat them as we have meat-eating—that is, institutionally discourage it but not make mandates.

Second, the church needs to consider its community responsibility in terms of its weaker members and evangelism. Both young people and newer members would be classified as the weaker members of the church body. They have not yet had much experience in reasoning from cause to effect the results of their decisions. It takes time, often years, for a person to settle into lifelong convictions as a result of their personal experiences. At some point we, as parents or spiritual guardians of those newborn in the faith, must let them make their own decisions and reap the natural results. Though this is hard to do, it is necessary if we want them to become mature Christians on their own. It is really a matter of faith and trust in God. As was the case with Jacob and Joseph, they often have to be removed from their overprotective environments in order to experience their own personal discovery of God.

It's like a friend of mine told me about the day he and his wife bade farewell to their two teenage boys as they went off to a boarding academy. They had been as faithful as they could in raising the boys in their home school, teaching them the principles of what it means to live for Christ. For years they had cooperated with God in building those human ships. Now they were sending them out to a vast ocean of tempting storms and trials. As they put the boys on the bus and stood there helplessly watching and waving as the vehicle pulled out of the station, my friend softly muttered, "May the best God win!"

Roger Dudley concludes his study by observing, "Both this study and Valuegenesis reveal that youth want the church to be a place where they do not have to park their brains. They want to be able— even encouraged—to think for themselves rather than having everything laid out for them. They desire dialog.

"While we as a church have had a good deal of focus on children and youth, investing in them our best resources, there is evidence to suggest that they are not encouraged (generally speaking) to evaluate critically their faith, to question it, to rethink it for themselves, or to personally redefine it" (p. 197). Then he adds this sobering comment: "It is not easy to design a church for today's youth, but if we want Adventism to be around tomorrow, we have no other option" (p. 199).

I have personally lived more than half of my life in the world. The remainder I have spent in the Adventist Church. Concerning my own young people I must confess that I would rather they continue their quest for God within the borders of the church and not outside of it, even if it means I must move outside my comfort zone to accommodate some of their desires to try out things that their mother and I don't necessarily agree with. Of course, I am talking here about youth who are past their most formative years. The time to train them is when they are small. As they get older we must play the role of a wise friend, gently counseling while allowing them to make their own choices. Just as it is with our evangelistic interests, a forceful, manipulative, overbearing attitude will never succeed in fully wedding a heart to the true Christ. Violating another's free will only misrepresents God. Each parent and teacher must seek Him for wisdom to know where to draw the line, ever recognizing the fine balance between idealism and realism.

Once again I painfully realize that some will be tempted to misconstrue my motives for what I have written, arguing that it is a subtle proposal to do away with the standards—but they miss the point. I'm a committed believer in the importance of standards. I just fear the danger of becoming like the Pharisees in that "their own attainments became the standard by which they judged others" (MB 123).

## A Final Word

Though this book has not dealt comprehensively with all the lifestyle issues confronting the Adventist Christian today, it has sought to bring to the forefront some of the things that seek to threaten church unity. Hopefully the principles discussed can be a useful tool in determining how we are to relate to other lifestyle issues facing the Christian. While realizing that we will never live as perfectly as Christ did, I think the true remnant who are truly seeking to be identified by His name will strive to pattern His example as closely as possible. But I also believe that they will take into consideration the needs and religious liberty of others along the way. As they grow in grace they will more and more display a compassionate attitude toward those who are "ignorant, and on them that are out of the way," thus "making a difference" in the lives of others (Heb. 5:2; Jude 22).

God's expectation, what He is trying to accomplish by incorporating lifestyle principles into our lives, is twofold. He designs that through them we shall bring honor to Him, while at the same time become better equipped to serve our fellow human beings. In doing this, we shall "render him the fruits in their seasons" (Matt. 21:41).

May God aid each one of us as we seek to live a lifestyle that will please Him, as well as one that will thoughtfully relate to those who do not yet know Him, or who are in the process of getting to know Him.